Teilhard de Chardin
SEVEN STAGES
OF SUFFERING

A Spiritual Path for Transformation

LOUIS M. SAVARY and
PATRICIA H. BERNE

Paulist Press
New York / Mahwah, NJ

Cover image by oldmonk/Shutterstock.com
Cover design and book design by Sharyn Banks

Library of Congress Cataloging-in-Publication Data

Savary, Louis M.
    Teilhard de Chardin - seven stages of suffering : a spiritual path for transformation / Louis M. Savary and Patricia H. Berne.
        pages cm
    Includes bibliographical references and index.
        ISBN 978-0-8091-4940-7 (pbk. : alk. paper) — ISBN 978-1-58768-531-6 (ebook)
        1. Suffering—Religious aspects—Christianity. 2. Teilhard de Chardin, Pierre. I. Title.
    BV4909.S295 2015
    248.8`6—dc23

                                                                          2014044330

ISBN 978-0-8091-4940-7 (paperback)
ISBN 978-1-58768-531-6 (e-book)

Published by Paulist Press
997 Macarthur Boulevard
Mahwah, New Jersey 07430

www.paulistpress.com

Printed and bound in the
United States of America

*This book is respectfully dedicated to the memory of
Pierre Teilhard de Chardin, SJ, who has been the inspiration
for almost everything we have written, taught, and believed.
He has given us new ways to understand God and evolving
creation, he has brought us to new levels of awareness
and consciousness, and he has even opened a new door to
our understanding of suffering.*

Contents

Preface

It is better to be healthy than sick.

Who could challenge that statement? Not even God would, and Jesus never refused to heal anyone. He never said to anyone who came to him for healing, "You deserve to be sick," or, "You deserve to live with that infirmity." Always he restored people to health.

No one wants to be in pain or to suffer unnecessarily. To be healthy is a universal desire. God wants you to be healthy and whole. It is important to emphasize that.

While we all want to be healthy, many of us are not. We suffer in many ways, and it seems such a waste!

However, the startling fact of God's plan for the human race is that even if you are sick or in some other way wounded or diminished by circumstances in your life, you can still effectively contribute to saving the world. You can do it through your suffering.

Teilhard de Chardin realized that suffering, at any and all stages of sickness or diminishment, can be transformed into a significant force for good. Your pain and suffering have the power to make a positive difference in the divine Spirit's grand project of renewing the face of the Earth.

Whether you have just left the doctor's office, having received for the first time a diagnosis of cancer, or whether you are enduring terminal pain during the last hours of your life on Earth in a hospice bed, your pain and suffering can become a transformative force.

The purpose of this book is to show you how your pain and suffering, like the pain and suffering of Jesus on the cross, can help us all move forward in consciousness and love.

—*Louis M. Savary and Patricia H. Berne*

Introduction

My sweet young niece, Sandy, the mother of two little girls, is dying of cancer.

My best friend, Nancy, beset with Lyme disease, has been waking up every morning for the past year with headache, nausea, back and neck pain, dizziness, and fatigue.

Daily, for the past eight years, Art, at eighty-four, has been visiting his wife with Alzheimer's in a nursing home. In anguish, he says, "No matter how hard I try to keep making a connection with Meg, she doesn't recognize me."

Alicia comes home each day after high school classes are over and is afraid to enter her house for fear of being physically abused by her alcoholic father. "I have lived many years of my life in fear of him, every day."

Dorothy, a grown woman and the youngest of seven, talks about her father dying of a brain tumor when she was only four. "Helplessly, my mother watched the man she loved die over many months, and when he died she raised her kids and ran the farm. I never knew her to have a day when she laughed. She spent the rest of her life deeply depressed."

When Gretchen and her friends get together, they compare their woes—arthritis, diabetes, constipation, headaches, lack of balance, high blood pressure, skin disease, bad eyesight, recovering from a stroke. The list of their pains and diminishments goes on and on.

Bob and Carol are raising their son Greg, who is wheelchair-bound with cerebral palsy. They have been doing it for twenty-two years.

Allan, back from a year of volunteer work in East Africa, tells a group of us, "You think you have suffering here. Where I

1

was stationed, most kids go to bed crying of hunger almost every night."

These are some of the stories of how people we know are diminished by pain and suffering. You must know people like them, too. Doesn't it make you wonder why people must suffer?

No matter where you turn, no matter where you look, suffering is everywhere.

When people are asked what they think of suffering and how they make sense of it, they offer a variety of responses.

Some are very pessimistic. They say that suffering has no meaning, no purpose; it is a waste of human life, and makes no sense.

Some are quite stoic. They say that whatever pain or suffering comes our way, we should just endure it as best we can and go on with life. Suffering happens, period!

Others say that we deserve to suffer in this life; it is punishment for our sins, or they say that suffering is God's way of testing our faith. "We should be like Jesus, who obediently suffered for us on the cross."

Others, at least in theory, believe that suffering can bring wisdom. They believe that God allows suffering so that we will learn important life lessons from it.

Each of us has our own way of trying to make sense of our own suffering and the pain and suffering of others.

Something New

In 1933, someone asked a French Jesuit priest, Pierre Teilhard de Chardin, to write an essay on the meaning of suffering. Teilhard, as we affectionately call him, was not only a theologian, he was a modern scientist who studied geology and the evolution of life on earth. He was also a deeply religious man—what we might label today "a mystic." Near the end of his essay, titled "The Meaning and Constructive Value of Suffering," he wrote these astounding words:

Human suffering, the sum total of suffering poured out at each moment over the whole earth, is like an immeasurable ocean. But what makes up this immensity? Is it blackness,

2

emptiness, barren wastes? No, indeed: it is potential energy. Suffering holds hidden within it, in extreme intensity, the ascensional force of the world.

The whole point is to set this force free by making it conscious of what it signifies and of what it is capable. For if all the sick people in the world were simultaneously to turn their sufferings into a single shared longing for the speedy completion of the kingdom of God through the organizing of the earth, what a vast leap toward God the world would thereby make![1]

In all the thinking and reading you may have done on the topic of suffering, have you ever encountered anything like the claims made in these two paragraphs? Teilhard's quotation summarizes the tremendous meaning and significance of the evolutionary energy produced daily by the human race—and groaning creation—yet hidden in the expenditure of pain and suffering. Everything in these pages flows from those two paragraphs, so read them again and again, ponder the revelations, and find comfort in what they may hold for you in your suffering.

This is not a book about dying or how to die. Rather, it is a book about how to live, specifically how to live positively and productively while enduring pain and suffering. As you noticed in some of the opening personal statements, you don't need to be sick to be suffering. This book is primarily about personal and collective spiritual growth in an evolving but suffering world.

Teilhard's seven stages of suffering[2] should not be confused with the typical stages of death and dying—denial, anger, bargaining, depression, and acceptance—as found in Elizabeth Kubler-Ross's classic text *On Death and Dying*. You do not have to be dying—or even sick—to progress to the highest stages of suffering, since there are many kinds of suffering that do not involve being ill or diseased. Pain and suffering may be found everywhere, not merely in a sickbed.

Two Primary Functions

In our evolutionary world, Teilhard tells us that those who suffer play a unique role. They have two primary functions: first, to pursue their own *personal spiritual growth*, and second, to direct the energy generated by their pain and suffering toward the *spiritual growth of humanity*.

Regarding the first primary function, all of us, even those weakened by disease or other diminishments, are challenged to develop ourselves and actualize ourselves, to become fully human. Within this personal spiritual growth process there are at least two sides to personal spiritual growth: first, *to keep growing in consciousness* of who we are in God's eyes, and, second, *to fulfill our life purpose*.

The second primary function of those who suffer is *to learn how to direct positively their suffering energy for building the kingdom of God*. Teilhard wants those who suffer to realize that their suffering generates significant potential energy. Sadly, many people see the energy they expend in their suffering as a waste. They do not realize that this energy can be used like fuel and directed, by their choice, to any effort, small or large, that would increase compassion, caring, or the advancement of life on earth.

Teilhard insists that we can use our suffering energy productively because we are all living in a Divine Milieu. Because we are all living in God's love—much like trillions of cells living in a human body—we are all connected and in communion with each other in that Divine Milieu. Thus, we can choose to use the energy we generate in our pain and suffering to support any person or project living and operating in that Divine Milieu.

The Divine Project

Regarding each one's unique life purpose, in a more traditional society it may have been enough to satisfy one's God-given purpose on earth by avoiding sin and thereby saving one's soul. In the evolutionary world in which we live, avoidance of sin is not enough to satisfy one's God-given purpose. God's challenge to each of us is to make as many positive contributions to the spiritual growth of the human race as we can, including our own spiritual growth. In this endeavor, each of us is called uniquely to make a positive difference in our world.

We are personally called by God to do whatever we can that would increase the consciousness of society; expand its care for the needy; multiply its compassion and forgiveness; spread its expressions of generosity and gratitude; deepen its tolerance for different ways of thinking; share its resources; bring about peace on earth; care for the environment; and make advances in health care, science, technology, governance, and other areas.

Although many sick and suffering people may no longer be able to be part of the daily active workforce in the offices, schools, factories, and research centers that are making a difference in our communities, these people can always contribute by living out their own life purpose actively, wherever they may be, in acts of compassion, kindness, caring, gratitude, forgiveness, and generosity.

Moreover, what has often been forgotten is that those who live in unavoidable pain may transform their suffering into energy in order to fuel some specific projects that are actively working to renew the face of the earth for God, for example, cancer research, feeding the poor and hungry, the cessation of terrorism, and so on.

This book shows Teilhard's *plan* for accomplishing God's *project,* which includes both personal spiritual growth and the spiritual growth of the human race. The divine project's goal of renewing Earth's face includes both personal and collective spiritual growth. Indeed, we pray for the fulfillment of this divine project—and agree to cooperate with it—when in the Lord's Prayer we say, *Thy will be done on Earth.*

The Seven Stages

Stages of Resistance. Teilhard suggests that spiritual growth in the suffering process typically begins with *resistance* to the illness, disease, or diminishment; it includes *outer* resistance (stage 1), as well as *inner* resistance (stage 2). Outer resistance might involve eating healthily, getting physical exercise, and taking prescribed medications. Inner resistance might involve thinking positively, praying, and finding quiet time. During these earliest stages, Teilhard advises you to avoid any suffering or diminishments you see coming; get out of their way, if possible. Do everything in your power to get rid of them or do something to change their power or potential. As long as human resistance is possible, Teilhard says, the total Body of Christ will be resisting with you. While God does not want anyone to suffer, God certainly wants your help in removing any diminishments that may threaten you. Furthermore, insofar as possible, you are expected to help God remove diminishments from others.

Stages of Transformation. Persons who realize they cannot be cured, despite their effort at resistance, enter what Teilhard calls a process of *transformation.* The objective of those who suffer at this stage becomes healing and wholeness, that is, living life fully despite illness or other forms of diminishment. In working through this transformation process, Teilhard focuses on the importance of *prayer, patience,* and *choice.* These comprise the themes of stages 3, 4, and 5. The challenge here is to acknowledge that your diminishments and unwelcome experiences are happening in the Divine Milieu. In every moment, whether in joy or in pain, you are continually loved by God. Nevertheless, as a created being you are still incomplete, and every other incomplete being is, at the same time, striving for its own completeness. With everyone around you striving, there are bound to be conflicts, competition, loss, and failure. Moreover, Earth itself and everything on it is still incomplete, still evolving, and still in a state of process. Yet in this process, God can transfigure our diminishments— even our physical deaths—by integrating them into a larger, better plan, says Teilhard, provided we lovingly trust God.

Suffering requires a tremendous expenditure of energy. It is important how you "direct" that energy. For example, you could do it negatively in anger toward God, or positively in union with God. During these stages of transformation, directing your suffering energy becomes centrally important. Learning how to redirect the energy of suffering positively is central to the stages of transformation. Perhaps you wish to direct your suffering energy to deepen a dying friend's faith in God, to bring reconciliation to your divided church congregation, to influence a drive raising funds to feed and clothe hurricane victims, or to encourage university research in discovering a cure for a new and dangerous viral infection.

Stages of Union. Finally, in these last two stages, Teilhard describes a very special process of spiritual growth. It begins where the suffering has taken over your life and is now inescapable, and where Teilhard says you are "resigned" to it. You fully accept it.

In this process of deep diminishment, Teilhard describes the two sides of the highest form of suffering spirituality—*personal spiritual growth* and the love of God (stage 6) and dedication to the *collective spiritual growth* of humanity and the love of creation (stage 7). It has been suggested that these final two stages be named as stages of *union* as a better way to characterize their emphasis on spiritual growth.

For each of the seven stages of suffering, we suggest appropriate *guiding principles*, *spiritual practices*, and *prayer forms*. The guiding principles and many of the suggestions for approaches to spiritual practices for each stage come directly from Teilhard's writings. Although the words of Teilhard's own prayers during times of his own suffering may be found scattered among his many essays, they are quite lengthy and written in his typical spontaneous and flowing way. Unfortunately, while the core of his personal prayers suggests beautiful ideas, we have chosen not to include many because they do not resonate, in their original form, with the words people use in prayer today. Consequently, most of the prayer forms included in the text have been newly created or have been adopted or adapted from other traditional and contemporary sources.[3]

Teilhard's Sufferings

In the realm of physical suffering, Teilhard dealt with heart problems, pleurisy, and insomnia for many years. However, his physical suffering was trifling compared to the emotional depression and spiritual anguish he endured at the hands of his Jesuit superiors and officials of the Roman Catholic Church.

Despite the harsh treatment he received from most of his brother Jesuits and fellow priests and despite the urging of many professional friends to leave the Society of Jesus and the Church, he remained obediently faithful to his religious vows, his order, and the church of his childhood and family.

After his priestly ordination and the popularity of his public lectures, the Holy Office in Rome, perhaps feeling threatened on how to deal with Teilhard's revolutionary and evolutionary ideas, ordered his Jesuit provincial to "exile" him from Paris. In this vibrant European center of new learning, young people were enthusiastic to hear his thoughts about integrating modern science and evolutionary theory into Christian theology. So, under pressure from Rome, he was sent on assignment to work at a Jesuit-run geological museum in China, where he was ordered to remain for twenty years, except for a very few short return visits to France to present scientific papers. Despite his many letters from China, begging his superiors to be allowed to return to his native land if only for an extended visit, he was consistently refused by Rome's demand.

During his exile in China, he writes in his daily journal of weeping at the rejection and cold treatment he felt from his Jesuit superiors and the official Church. In his repeated attempts and revisions to get approval for publication of his book, *The Divine Milieu*—what he called "a simple book of piety"—he was refused any access to meetings with Vatican officials to discuss difficult issues with his manuscripts or teachings. Many of his insights on suffering may be found in *The Divine Milieu*.

Everyone began leaving China after the Communist takeover following World War II. Upon his return, Teilhard was able to spend a few years in France, during which time he was not allowed to speak in public on theology. He was told to find employment outside of Europe. He was expelled from France, forbidden to return. His concerned anthropological colleagues found a job for him in New York City at the Wenner-Gren Foundation, reviewing grants for anthropological research in Africa.

When he came to live and work in New York City, he at first lived in a Jesuit house; there, he reports being consistently avoided by his fellow Jesuits. Shortly after, he was asked to move out and find his own living quarters. He spent his final years in a residential hotel room, with a single window looking out into a sunless alley.

He died without any of his books or theological essays being published. When his body was delivered for burial to the Jesuit novitiate in Poughkeepsie, New York, where his remains are kept, he did not receive the usual honors of a faithful Jesuit, but was buried without ceremony in a grave with a stone that did not even have his full name engraved on it.

Fortunately, Teilhard bequeathed all of his manuscripts to his secretary, Jeanne Mortier, who had devotedly kept his papers in order for many years. It was she who offered them to a Paris publisher.

Thanks to her, we have his two major books, *The Divine Milieu* and *The Phenomenon of Man*, plus eight more, each of which is a collection of his letters and essays.

He turned the energy of depression and rejection into his own work for the kingdom of God. During his years of exile in China, since he was not physically disabled, he directed his energy to scholarly publications—over fifteen hundred of them—and his spiritual writing. Furthermore, in his last year in New York, when he had become severely weakened physically, he used his remaining energy to continue writing letters and essays explaining his evolutionary ideas. He was always striving to make a positive difference with his life. He never gave up. In fact, through his writings and his life, it can be seen that he had reached the highest stages of suffering.

Essential
Perspectives

Most of us are used to taking a very short-range and personal view of suffering. The pain is happening to me and I want to know why. Who is to blame for my suffering? If I can't find someone to blame, I ask, "Why me?" or, "Why did God let this happen to me?"

A much larger perspective is to realize that we are living in an evolving world. Furthermore, over the centuries, even while widespread suffering continues to happen, dedicated people have been improving humanity's ability to understand the sources of suffering, learning how to deal with them, and alleviating some of the pain they cause.

For example, at the time of Jesus the average human life span was somewhere around thirty years, most likely due to lack of proper nutrition, harsh weather, and scores of illnesses and infections that had no cure at the time. At the beginning of the twentieth century, the average person lived about fifty or sixty years. Today, that figure is around eighty years.

Medicine has created antiseptics, antibiotics, and vaccines to prevent, cure, and in some cases, eliminate many diseases that were among the highest causes of death during the twentieth century.

For people with heart problems, many new advances have been made with stents, coronary bypasses, pacemakers, and even heart transplants. Many older people are taking a daily baby aspirin to help prevent heart attacks. For those with high blood pressure, preventive measures and medications are readily available.

For victims of limb loss, especially during war times, the science of prosthetics has made great advances.

Genetics and gene therapy provide great new frontiers in the field of medicine.

Great strides have been made in medicine to help manage certain mental illnesses and develop forms of therapy to treat depression, anxiety, grief, and trauma.

People are much better informed about illnesses and ways to prevent them than ever before. There are chat rooms on the Internet for people with the same illness to share their stories, their treatments, their hopes, and to offer support to one another.

However, while modern science and medicine keep finding new ways to alleviate human suffering, there seems to be no shortage of situations that cause people to suffer physically, emotionally, and spiritually.

Improvements in communication allow us to become aware of unattended suffering in other parts of the world. At the same time, improvements in transportation allow new infectious diseases to travel everywhere in the world on people's bodies, clothing, or in the luggage items they carry with them. No matter how much precaution is taken at national borders or customs stations, new problems that create suffering manage to get by and spread their unwanted effects.

Increasing population, endless violent clashes all over the planet, climate change, food shortages, water shortages, illegal drug trafficking, terrorism, hunger, and poverty create mounting challenges for governments and other organizations committed to reducing the suffering of humanity.

Despite the fact that tremendous strides have been taken to reduce human suffering, and efforts to alleviate human anguish continue onward, we are still living in an unfinished world filled with pain, frustration, loss, grief, and adversity. How can those who suffer live with and understand their pain? Is it possible that those who suffer can become coworkers with God in bringing our world to more fullness of life, even as they suffer?

Because Teilhard personally suffered much, not only physically, but also emotionally and spiritually, it was important for him to find some purpose and significance for suffering in God's plan. Teilhard found a way that we humans—even those of us who suffer—can help foster, promote, and contribute to God's work in the world.

Being both an evolutionary scientist and a theologian, Teilhard had a number of significant insights or realizations related to pain and

suffering that form the foundational ideas for understanding the evolutionary stages of responding to your pain and suffering.

Foundational Insights

1. Pain and Suffering Are Inevitable and Unavoidable in Our Evolving World.

An evolving world is inevitably an unfinished world and an
imperfect world, even in this twenty-first century. Clearly, we have
not yet reached the mental, emotional, and spiritual maturity
required for the human race to live together in loving unity—as one
great healthy and happy family caring for one another. Suffering and
diminishments are still inescapable in our present world.

Much of the daily suffering people undergo is unintentional
and unavoidable, primarily because we live in such a crowded, complex, and unfinished world. For example, because our genetic
makeup is so incredibly intricate and delicate, it is inevitable that in
some cases during conception a gene may make a small copying
error or fail to duplicate itself completely, and a child will be born
with some genetic defect or deficiency, such as cerebral palsy or mus-
cular dystrophy, or a proneness to certain physical or mental illnesses
such as heart disease, cancer, or Alzheimer's disease.

Environmental factors may create or intensify certain illnesses
or diseases, such as asthma or diabetes. Socioeconomic factors such
as poverty or drug-infested neighborhoods may generate suffering in
the form of fear, frustration, and anguish. Parental upbringing spring-
ing from a habit of abuse, mistrust, violence, anger, or greed may nur-
ture destructive attitudes and beliefs in children that cause discomfort
and pain throughout life. Consequently, children, having little or no
power to change such circumstances, suffer from them.

From humanity's earliest age, and even today, people everywhere on Earth have suffered while struggling against the elements
of nature—not only wind and rain, hurricanes and tornadoes, floods
and droughts, but also scarcity of food and housing, and various bacteria and viruses fighting to impress their way of life upon us.
Although meteorologists may sometimes be able to predict the

approach of oncoming natural disasters, they cannot prevent them. Medicine, too, is only slowly, step-by-step, learning how to respond to various illnesses and diseases.

Much pain and suffering is generated by the ordinary, unwelcome diminishments that we endure in life—and can do little about—due to social and economic inequality. No one gets to choose where and when they are born. While some are born in highly industrialized nations, many more are born in underdeveloped countries, where medicine, safe drinking water, education, and opportunities for advancement are woefully lacking. Even in prosperous nations, while a small percentage of the population may control 80 percent of the wealth, many will suffer unemployment or underemployment, work for wages that are insufficient to raise their families, and live in painful poverty or even homelessness.

This suffering does not come from God, but from humanity's immaturity. Although we have evolved significantly from our cave-dwelling eras, we are still far from mature as a species. God is not punishing us, says Teilhard, but calling us to evolve.

Of course, we sometimes cause our own suffering or we cause suffering in others by our greed, cruelty, jealousy, and pride, our wanting to be first or to have more power. In revenge, we may want to cause grief and pain to others. Many of us are still emotionally and spiritually undeveloped, so we unconsciously support—and do little to lessen our exposure to—violence and cruelty in the world. As nations and communities, we declare war on each other in the mistaken belief that violence can somehow bring peace, when all it brings is more domination.

Although pain and suffering and other diminishments are inevitable and unavoidable in our evolving planet, God is not the cause of our suffering. Neither can God prevent all suffering and diminishment in a world still in process, especially within a still immature humanity. In this context, Teilhard asks us to take a new perspective on what God is trying to do in and with creation.

Teilhard suggests that it is far more beneficial to ask the following: What is this divine project? How does it work? What is our role in it? And how does suffering fit in?

2. We Are Called to Actively Participate in the Accomplishment of God's Evolutionary Project.

God started this divine evolutionary project at the first moment of creation almost fourteen billion years ago, and the grand project is still evolving, and still very incomplete. A loving planet is the goal of the evolutionary process. We are in the midst of it, on the journey, and we are meant to be workers with God—and all the other creatures—in bringing about the fulfillment of this divine project.

Our responsibility in helping complete God's project for Earth is most clearly expressed in the Lord's Prayer, when we affirm our commitment to that divine project saying, "Thy will be done on Earth."

God's project is being driven by *an evolutionary law*. At the first moment of creation, at the big bang, when nothing was yet organized—not even into simple atoms or molecules—and all that existed was a chaotic explosion of subatomic particles, God placed a law of love into every one of those particles. That law still lives and operates in all the elements and creatures that have evolved since the big bang. Teilhard gave definition to that creative law of divine love as the Law of Attraction-Connection-Complexity-Consciousness.[1] It simply means that all things are *attracted* to one another and driven to form *connections* and relationships; these connections become more and more complex, as creation evolves from atoms to molecules to cells to organisms to plants to animals to humans. To understand these creatures and their increasing *complexity*, we need to develop higher and higher levels of awareness and *consciousness*. As we work with this law, we will keep evolution and God's project moving forward and upward toward its fulfillment.

This law was a significant discovery of Teilhard's. However, he reminds us that diminishments will continue to happen along the way, for suffering and diminishments are inevitable in an unfinished world.

3. Human Suffering as Well as Human Work Generate Energy for God's Project.

For us to work on God's project, what Jesus called building the kingdom of God, requires *energy*, which is defined as "the ability to do work."

Much of our human energy is expended in our consciously chosen activities, our work and professions. These are physical and mental efforts that are designed to improve the world and help achieve the divine project. Our daily work energy is effective because the intention behind our work is to make a better world, to help bring about God's kingdom on Earth. Our intention makes the difference. Our intention and our choices direct the energy we produce in our positive efforts to help build the Body of Christ.

On the other hand, much of our human energy is also expended in suffering—physical, emotional, and spiritual suffering. The most important insight Teilhard had about suffering was that suffering generates energy. It requires energy, sometimes tremendous energy, to endure pain and suffering. Furthermore, since energy is the ability to do work, Teilhard suggests that the sufferer could redirect this energy toward doing the work of building the Body of Christ—wherever that energy was most needed.

Just as we sometimes waste time doing nothing, we can also waste energy—and suffering energy is probably the easiest energy to waste. We waste suffering energy when we see it simply as something that has no use or value, or must simply be endured, or as a punishment. When we treat suffering energy as useless and undesirable, it gets wasted. But it doesn't have to be so.

Just as I may choose how to invest my money, my financial savings, by my intention and choice, I may also choose how to invest my energy, generated in my labor and suffering by my intention and choice.

Teilhard wants us to invest the energy we generate in suffering as if it were fuel—like coal, oil, natural gas, or solar energy. We can take the potential energy locked up in any fuel or the sun and either use it in productive ways or waste it. We make it productive by channeling it. We channel it by our choice. Likewise, our suffering energy is potential energy. We need to direct it, to channel it, and thereby make it useful in helping renew the face of the Earth.

Can the energy produced in suffering—by our intention and choice—also help build the Body of Christ on earth? Teilhard informs us how we can learn to use our suffering creatively and productively, and he encourages us personally to direct the "energy" of our suffering to someone or some project that we care about and that needs our support.

Teilhard believed that Jesus in the Garden of Gethsemane and on the cross was "directing the intense energy of his suffering" toward the growth of love in the world. In this perspective, rather than seeing his passion and death as an act simply to atone for humanity's sin, Teilhard suggests that Jesus' suffering also has a constructive evolutionary meaning and purpose. So Teilhard presents a practical, productive, and creative spirituality of the cross.

4. There Is Only One Christian Spirituality— The Spirituality of the Cross.

The classical spirituality of Christ's suffering and death on the cross is focused primarily on how Christ graciously suffered to save us from our sins and from final damnation. In this view, redemption is primarily a merciful forgiving, protective, and preventive action for fallen humanity.

In Teilhard's view, which includes and goes beyond the classical view, Christ's suffering energy is also life giving. That is, his suffering not only saved us from the worst of the negative forces but, on the cross, Christ was also *modeling a constructive (evolutionary) approach to suffering.* The energy released through Jesus' suffering not only kept us from a final devolution into sin and death, but nurtured us into a fuller potential life in him.

Christ on the cross taught us how to use even the diminishment forces of life, including suffering, to make a positive difference in the lives of our fellow humans and the planet.

Think of Jesus' suffering energy as having two phases, *redemption* and *salvation.* In its first phase, *redemption*—Jesus' suffering energy—might be described as moving us from a state of sin to a state of forgiveness, thereby taking us from a negative state to zero— from financial loss or bankruptcy to a break-even point. To use another image, before our redemption we had been drowning and Jesus pulled us up out of the water and onto shore. This describes the classical position of why Christ died on the cross.

Why stop at zero? In an evolutionary world, Teilhard tells us that Christ has a much more positive objective for his suffering, something much more than redemption, namely, God's grand evolutionary project. In this more positive sense, in *salvation*, which means "giving us the fullness of life," Christ calls us to move from zero upward, to invest and use our assets—the energy produced by our work efforts and in our suffering—to help move the Body of Christ to an ever more profitable and mature state. To use the drowning image again, at this life-giving stage, Jesus doesn't just save us from drowning and leave us on the shore, he brings us back into the community and gives us jobs that use our talents. His suffering is not only lifesaving; it is also life giving.

In this second phase, Christ's suffering also releases energy in us for constructing a universe of loving union. He teaches us, "No one has greater love than this, to lay down one's life for one's friends." In such a loving death, one dies not only to preserve the lives of others, *but that those others may go on living constructively, that they may have life and have it in abundance.*

In reflecting on this idea, people can learn to direct, as Jesus did, the potential energy in the suffering they may be called upon to endure. They can direct it toward their own growth and healing as well as toward that of others. This is a way in which they can imitate Jesus in his positive use of suffering energy.

Enriched with a new perspective on suffering from these insights of Teilhard, and based on the ideas of St. Paul,[2] we can more accurately and profitably explore Teilhard's seven stages of suffering.

The Significance of Suffering

Having explored Teilhard's foundational insights regarding suffering, we observed, first, that he regarded pain and suffering as inevitable and unavoidable in our evolving, but unfinished world. Second, he suggested that God has initiated an ongoing evolutionary project—God's project—for transforming the world; that this divine project is being driven by God's love for creation, and that we humans are called to be engaged as partners with God in carrying out this project. Third, Teilhard showed how the energy for our part in this project comes not only from our physical efforts at home and in the workplace but also from the energy produced by our suffering. Finally, Teilhard introduced us to a more complete way of viewing Christ's suffering, a way that invites us to enjoy an ever-increasing fullness of life on Earth. With this understanding of these insights, we may now begin to focus on the meaning and significance of human suffering.

However, before exploring the seven stages of suffering, we must examine three additional insights that apply specifically to the stages of suffering.

Insights into Suffering

1. Suffering Is Broadly Defined

Although people may read this book because they are in physical pain from some illness or disease, human suffering is not always about illness, nor is it always physical. Because suffering—or "diminishment," to use Teilhard's language—may arise in many different ways, these seven stages may apply to a wide range of human suffering—physical, emotional, mental, spiritual, social, and occupational.

To mention just a few examples other than illness and disease, suffering can come from loneliness, unemployment, emotional rejection, incarceration, failure, grief, loss, poverty, homelessness, war, trauma, birth defects, financial insecurity, divorce, life transitions, midlife crisis, having nowhere to turn, a lack of acceptance by peers or family, getting fired, a failure to live up to expectations, abuse, unfulfilled longings, a loss of faith, a loss of hope, being an object of hatred or bullying, being unable to provide for one's family, despairing, being overwhelmed by problems, experiencing a lack of friends—and the list of the sources of suffering goes on.

Furthermore, the suffering that you experience may also come, not from any personal illness or crisis of your own, but from the heartbreak you feel when you observe compassionately the sufferings of others. This too is suffering because you expend energy in your compassion for others—for instance, watching children or grownups that are in pain from sickness or disease and not being able to help them or change their situation. You may feel bad for negative things happening to others, such as seeing your children not achieve well in school because of bullying or bad companionship; watching a loved one slowly dying in pain; living with a child or friend struggling with drug addiction or alcoholism; visiting in a nursing home, day after day, a long-time spouse with Alzheimer's who does not recognize you; or watching news reports of people being murdered or sexually assaulted. This compassionate suffering is also a powerful source of energy.

Furthermore, if you look at creation from an evolutionary perspective, creation itself has always been struggling and suffering. It is omnipresent on our planet Earth. From humanity's earliest age, people, animals, trees, and plants have struggled helplessly against the elements of nature. Science is only slowly, step-by-step, learning how to respond to various illnesses, diseases, and natural disasters. In Teilhard's words, "The self-organization of the world progresses only by dint of countless attempts to grope its way."[1]

2. Inflicting Pain or Harm on Yourself

This second insight is an important directive regarding self-inflicted suffering. As Teilhard notes, there are enough factors in the world that diminish us without having to inflict pain on ourselves. His seven stages of responding to suffering apply specifically to *unavoidable* suffering, not self-caused pain. He notes that self-caused pain or discomfort is usually avoidable. He recommends avoidance whenever suffering is avoidable.[2]

From a different perspective, if you are suffering from a disease that has medicine or treatment available, or a helpful activity that would help relieve some or all of your pain, Teilhard would advise you to use it, as he did for his heart problems, pleurisy, and insomnia.

Furthermore, suppose there is a medication available for your disease but you cannot afford it because of its high financial cost. Teilhard would tell you to keep trying to find a way to access that needed medicine, rather than continuing to endure suffering caused by your disease or ailment. Perhaps you might telephone the pharmaceutical company that makes it to see if you can negotiate with them, or you might approach your medical provider or insurer and ask them for alternative medications. For example, when Teilhard couldn't find the medicine that helped his insomnia in the United States, he had it shipped to him from Paris. The point is to keep working toward your health.

As a member of a religious order, Teilhard would also have been aware of other sources of self-inflicted suffering for religious reasons. It was not uncommon historically in Christian spirituality for individuals, especially monks and nuns, to engage in self-inflicted pain as a way of "participating" in the sufferings of Jesus. They might do this by wearing hair shirts, wrapping sharply pointed chains around their legs and waists, or whipping themselves with knotted cords. Such self-induced pain was seen traditionally as a devout spiritual practice, often regarded as a self-imposed penance for one's sins or as a way of testing oneself to see if one was willing to suffer for Christ. Others chose to do extreme fasting or other forms of illness-producing deprivation—for example, sleeping on cold floors or using other forms of self-torture, apparently as ways of identifying with Jesus' sufferings on the cross. Such penitential practices were common in religious orders before Vatican II. Even today, in some countries during Lent, flagellants walk on public streets whipping themselves, often drawing blood.

Many of these self-imposed penance practices ended up causing infections, pneumonia, early arthritis, and other crippling illnesses. Teilhard, who was probably required to perform some of these penitential practices as a young Jesuit, came to realize that harming oneself was not what Jesus or God is asking of us. Jesus himself believed this basic rule of avoiding avoidable pain. In the Garden of Gethsemane on the night before his passion, Jesus prayed to his Father that if this cup of suffering that looked imminent was not absolutely necessary, he would rather not choose it.

Today, there are many people who choose to inflict unnecessary suffering upon themselves. Although they do not flagellate themselves or wear skin-piercing chains, they do manage to harm their health with smoking, overeating, doing no exercise, starving themselves through anorexia or bulimia, consuming excessive amounts of alcohol or drugs, overwork, sleep deprivation, and so on.

Teilhard's point is that your primary purpose in life is to contribute in your unique way to God's evolutionary project. Almost always, the best way to serve your purpose on Earth is by being healthy. Teilhard asks, "For what is sanctity in a creature if not to adhere to God with the maximum of his strength?"[3]

Even while striving to maintain the best of health, people are still subject to things or events that diminish them. You may pick up a bacterial infection while visiting someone in the hospital. You may be a victim in an auto accident. Just don't consciously and willfully bring suffering upon yourself. Rather, keep working for your health—and that of others.

Teilhard's reasoning is that you and all those around you can probably do more for the kingdom of God if you have your health, than if you let yourself become a burden on yourself or others when you don't have to.

3. Redirecting Your Suffering Energy

This is a most crucial piece of Teilhard's insights into the significance of suffering and how we can avoid wasting its powerful energy. *During any of Teilhard's seven stages of suffering, you can always intentionally choose to direct the energy you spend in suffering toward some cause or purpose that would help improve the world.*

This principle also applies to the energy expended in temporary pain, as in a headache, a stiff neck, a bloated stomach, a bout of nausea, a night of insomnia, or the frustration of waiting in a long line. Such temporary suffering need not be wasted. It can always be transformed and made useful. As a general principle, says Teilhard, Christians know that their "function is to divinize the world in Jesus Christ."[4] For Teilhard, this principle applies in every situation. Your suffering, wherever and whenever, can function to help divinize the world.

There are many ways to redirect and make your suffering beneficial to others. In directing your suffering energy, there are three basic options.

First, you can choose to direct your energy toward a general purpose, such as peace in the world, the eradication of hunger, respect for human life, or some other major issue that concerns you.

Second, you can choose to direct your suffering energy toward a particular or specific purpose, such as the health of a certain person, the success of a dangerous surgical procedure, a healthy pregnancy for a friend, achievement of a certain scientific venture, the success of a fundraising campaign for medical research, the safety of a worker on a volunteer team in a war-torn country, and so on. In some ways, psychologists tell us, the more focused your intention, the more likely you are to use your energy productively and not waste it.

Third, if you have no particular focus for your suffering energy, you may simply present it to Christ or to the Creator to be used for whatever is needed at the moment to move God's project forward. Teilhard's point is that rather than waste your suffering energy, at whatever stage of suffering you may be, there is always someone or some place that can use your energy.

You can also make a general offering of your suffering each morning, with the intention of applying all your energy, whether it is generated by your work or by your suffering. Furthermore, you can reaffirm your intention each time you become aware of pain or suffering surfacing. Some people find a traditional image of the Sacred Heart of Jesus as a way of offering, each morning, all of their actions and all of their sufferings for the healing of the world.

However, do not fall into the trap of consciously increasing your suffering, as if it were better to suffer than to be free of what causes you to suffer.

A Universal Spiritual Practice

This is a spiritual practice to be used during all seven stages of suffering. You begin with the guiding principle and attitude that your pain and suffering, in whatever form you experience it, is not a waste of energy, but through your choice can become a powerful force for good.

An essential insight of Teilhard is that your suffering has meaning and significance because it is a source of energy that may be directed in positive ways for a *specific purpose*. With this attitude, here are some suggested steps:

1. Use your imagination to give form and shape to your suffering as a kind of fuel or force that, as potential energy, needs to be directed or channeled to accomplish some specific result. For example, you may picture your suffering energy as a beam of sunlight, a current of electricity, a gust of wind, or an arrow you are shooting at a target.
2. Select the target, that is, the person(s) or project toward which you wish to aim or direct your suffering energy, and picture in detail the result you wish to help accomplish. (Some desired results may need tremendous amounts of energy, require repeated applications of energy, or energy from many different people.)
3. By your conscious choice, release your energy and use your imagination to direct it, such as a beam of light or arrow, toward the person(s) or project you have chosen.
4. Thank God that you can be of service in healing the human family, even though you are sick or diminished in some other way.

Our suggestion is to redirect your energy toward an objective that you can clearly picture in your mind. The more concrete and specific you make the recipient of your energy, the more satisfying it will be. Practice on simpler things before you choose something immense to manifest, like peace on earth.

For example, a retired teacher of handicapped children, suffering from Parkinson's disease, found a natural way to begin practicing this spiritual activity. She chose to direct her suffering energy to healing the children she knew best. She said,

> Today I am directing all my suffering energy to bless the children born blind, who don't get to see the beauties of nature, their mothers' smile, the faces of all those who love them, or all the colors and shapes surrounding them.
>
> Tomorrow I will direct all my suffering energy to bless the children born deaf, who don't know their parents' voice, don't hear their parents singing lullabies, don't hear the serenades of birds, or can't play a musical instrument.

Here are three other stories of sufferers redirecting their energy toward the healing of others:

> I am a hospital nurse with constant headaches that no painkillers seem to touch. So, what I do is choose a patient on my floor who has a terminal disease and focus all my suffering energy for his or her healing. This helps keep me conscious that I can use my own suffering energy to do some specific good, and not just complain about my headaches.

* * *

> I am in prison for a crime I didn't commit, which creates a lot of suffering for me, knowing that I could be living a happy, ordinary life, raising a family and all the rest. But here I am, with a few years yet to serve. I discovered that there are a lot of guys in this prison, not because they are criminals, but because they are mentally ill and being treated like criminals—and they are helpless to do anything about either their illness or their conviction. Other

prisoners sometimes treat them cruelly precisely because they are so vulnerable. I direct my suffering energy for the safety and peace of mind of these mentally sick guys.

* * *

I am a veteran who lost both my legs in the war. I wear prostheses but I still have a lot of physical pain. Most of my pain is emotional, however, because I am frustrated that I cannot do with my boys all the activities I would like to do as their father. I also feel embarrassed because the friends that my kids bring home all stare at my prostheses. I have lots of suffering energy to contribute to the healing of the world. I choose to focus my energy on the families—especially the kids—in those foreign countries who lose their homes and their loved ones to the destructive effects of war. Whenever I see photos of devastation on television, I say to God, "Take my suffering energy and make it healing energy for the family in that photo." It's the only way I can watch war news and not just cry in anguish at the uselessness of the violence we unleash on our fellow human beings.

Others have focused the healing capacity of their suffering energy on, for example, the homeless people in their hometown; women considering an abortion today; people seeking jobs unsuccessfully this day; weaker parties being taken advantage of in divorce proceedings; innocent people escaping from their terrorized homes seeking political asylum and yet being treated as criminals in our country; immigrant farm workers who do back-breaking labor picking produce that we enjoy at our dinner tables and are paid barely subsistence wages; elderly people with dementia in nursing homes who are left to suffer and treated as if they were subhuman; children and spouses who are physically and sexually abused daily by their own family members; people suffering from addictions who seem unable to respond to treatment; and people who live in countries where there is daily fear of ethnic violence, terrified that it will erupt at any moment, triggered by the wrong word uttered at the wrong time.

Part One

STAGES OF RESISTANCE

One common response to the approach of suffering would tell you to accept it as part of life. "Suffering happens. Get used to it." A religious variation on this response might be, "Suffering happens. Just offer it up," or "Jesus suffered for your sake, so why shouldn't you suffer, too?" Another religious response tells you to consider your pain and suffering as a punishment you probably deserve for something you did to offend God. Some even say that God allows us to suffer so that we will learn important lessons about life from it, such as patience, compassion, and wisdom. Others tell you that human suffering has no real significance, purpose, or meaning, but you must endure it.

Teilhard rejects all of these "helpless" and "passive" responses to suffering, especially during the earliest stages of illness or signs of diminishment. When it looks like pain and suffering are approaching—for example, at the first signs or symptoms of a cold or flu, the earliest onset of a disease, or the likelihood of some form of personal diminishment, like loss of a job, rejection of a friend, or a major life change—Teilhard says to resist it and fight it like an enemy.

> At the first approach of diminishments we cannot hope to find God except by loathing what is coming upon us and doing our best to avoid it. The more we repel suffering at that moment, with our whole heart and our whole

strength, the more closely we cleave to the heart and action of God.[1]

The reason Teilhard rejects these traditional explanations is because, for him, God's nature and very name is *Love*. By that definition, God must wish for all of us to enjoy the fullness of life. Any less of a wish would be to contradict the infinitely loving nature of God. For this reason alone, Teilhard would tell us to resist the approaching illness, fight the onset of a disease, prevent any immanent diminishment of your life, and avoid any sickness or infection.

Why? Because resisting is exactly what any loving parent would want you to do, and certainly what a loving God would want you to do. For Teilhard, any other response from God to a sign of oncoming pain or suffering for you would be "to deny the loving nature of God." After all, Jesus never was known to say to any suffering person who came to him for healing, "I refuse to heal you," or "You deserve this illness." In the Gospels, Jesus never approved of suffering. On the contrary, whenever Jesus saw suffering, it evoked his compassion and mercy. In his combating of sickness and suffering, Jesus was reflecting a God of love.

Teilhard would also remind you that this loving God has a grand plan for Earth that has been evolving for billions of years, and that each of us needs to make our unique contribution to that project during our special time on Earth. That is why we are alive here and now. Most likely, you and I can make our unique contribution more effectively and efficiently if we are not burdened by pain and suffering.

Why else would Jesus have performed so many healings? He had no need to use these healings to prove his divinity. In these healings, he was curing sick people and giving them back to their families and communities with health, so they could once again be productive individuals in their communities, not merely burdens to others or outcasts of society.

However, in any evolutionary process, Teilhard reminds us, there are bound to be mistakes, confusion, errors, losses, sickness, and death. All these many forms of diminishment we experience as humans are inevitable. People do get sick, some lose their jobs, and others are born with defects. Accidents occur often with unwelcome consequences. Wars are declared and people destroy lives and villages. Furthermore, nature itself, in its own developmental processes, produces violence in earthquakes, tornadoes, fires, and floods that cause additional human suffering. We are a long way from the evolutionary maturity God desires for us. The human family has not yet become the all-embracing, all-forgiving community that God calls us to be. Everything in creation is still struggling to evolve. As a human race, we are still on the way, still immature, and only slowly moving forward. There is still much suffering we must endure on the way. How are we to deal with it? That is the question Teilhard poses to himself.

His first two stages both focus on resisting suffering, avoiding it, preventing it, and seeking a cure for it whenever possible, by using inner resistance and outer resistance.

Stage 1 emphasizes *outer resistance*. This includes using any and all physical efforts to keep illness or diminishment at bay and to pursue an effective cure—the use of diet, exercise, and medications; avoiding infection; seeking pertinent information, appropriate medical care, and clinical testing to detect illness at its earliest stages; and making wise choices for behavioral ways to prevent potential infection or other forms of harm.

Stage 2 emphasizes *inner resistance*. This includes developing your intellectual and spiritual capacities to resist sources of pain and suffering. These mental tools include your inner attitudes and knowledge, imaginative imagery, mindfulness, and your beliefs about God, evolution, and the significance and meaning of suffering.

Obviously, these first two stages of suffering represent the two sides of resistance—inner and outer—which interact and support one another. So, at the first sign of pain and suffering approaching, we are to resist with all our strength using the power of God's loving spirit that lives within us.

If our resistance is successful—if the disease is cured or the diminishment averted—we can rejoice. However, if our resistance is not enough to keep the disease or diminishment from its approach, then Teilhard, in future stages, offers ways to transform the energy we expend in our pain and suffering into something significant, into something that will help further God's plan for humanity.

These early stages show how unique and fresh Teilhard's approach to suffering really is. He says that although suffering is indeed an unavoidable fact of life, we need not simply accept it helplessly when we see it coming. Rather, at the approach of suffering or any form of diminishment, we are to fight it and resist with all our strength because God wants us to be free of it. Furthermore, God is working through the evolutionary forces to make it happen.

Finally, if the diminishment is already happening to you, the advantage is that it can be named and its focal issue identified. For example, if it is a physical illness, such as diagnosis of a serious disease, you may choose to act in a certain way, such as ordering and taking any prescribed medications. If the diminishment is emotional, such as being the recipient of bullying or other verbal cruelty, you may choose to act in a different way, such as avoiding those places or situations where such cruelty is likely to occur. If it is a spiritual diminishment, such as fear, loss of faith, or despair, you may choose to act in helpful ways, such as seeking spiritual counseling or turning to supportive and understanding friends. There is value in knowing.

Stage 1

Outer Resistance

*Before the diminishment occurs or when it is likely to occur, resist
sickness, evil, and other diminishments with all your strength.*

This first stage of suffering might include someone who has just
received an initial diagnosis of an illness, infection, or disease from a
physician; someone who has just been in an auto accident or suffered
an occupational injury, but does not yet know the extent of their
diminishment; someone who has just heard that their marriage partner wants a divorce; a young person who has been verbally abused
by a parent but suspects that the abuse may escalate into physical
abuse; a person or family about to be evicted from their home; a student beginning to be bullied by a classmate; an employee about to be
laid off from work; or an undocumented immigrant about to be
deported. All of these people are suffering, and are called to fight.

During this stage of "outer resistance," Teilhard offers a number
of *guiding principles* and *spiritual practices* for our consideration. We also
suggest some appropriate *prayer forms* for this stage.

Guiding Principles

1. God Detests This Sickness or Diminishment.

God wants you to have life and to have it in abundance. In
Teilhard's own words, "To struggle against evil and to reduce to a
minimum even the ordinary physical evil which threatens us, is
unquestionably the first act of our Father who is in heaven; it would
be impossible to conceive him in any other way, and still more
impossible to love him."[1]

Teilhard asserts that removing diminishments from us must be "the first act" of our God whose name is Love. How else could we think of an all-loving, all-embracing divine Parent except in wanting to remove all sickness and diminishment from us? If this were not so, he says, it would be impossible for us to passionately love a divine Creator who preferred to treat us the way a cold-hearted parent might, watching us suffer and doing nothing about it—or even making us suffer.

2. Resist Suffering
Because God Wants You To.

Teilhard says, "We shall have to begin by saying, 'God wants to free me from this diminishment.'"[2] This is the starting point: we resist suffering because God wants us to.

However, despite all efforts at resistance, there is still much suffering. People still get sick. People still live with chronic illness. People still die of disease. People still get maimed and die in auto accidents. Babies continue to be born with deformities and disabilities. People still live in abusive households. People still endure diminishments like physical disabilities, poverty, homelessness, joblessness, loneliness, disease, epidemics, war, terrorism, and other forms of destruction. The planet is covered with a thousand forms of suffering. So, how can Teilhard say that God's "first act" is removing diminishment from us?

Teilhard might answer by pointing out that God did not create a perfect world, but a perfectible world. It is a world in evolution. It began in a chaotic state at the big bang, but God imbued those chaotic originating subatomic elements with a law urging and even driving everything toward a world of loving order.

Furthermore, those trillions of original subatomic particles have come a long way in their self-organization over almost fourteen billion years. While death must remain an inevitable fact in any evolving, physical universe—otherwise there could be no evolutionary development—we have learned many ways to alleviate suffering through God's inspiration and the divinely implanted evolutionary law driving us.

3. Acknowledge That God Wants Your Help in Removing This Diminishment from You.

Teilhard says, "God wants me to help him to take this cup from me."[3] As St. Ignatius once paradoxically advised, "Pray as if everything depended on God, and act as if everything depended on you."

Each year, we learn better how to deal with the diseases and illnesses that diminish us. We have developed methods and products for safety. We have social systems, though still inadequate, to care for the poor, the homeless, the orphans, the hungry, and the elderly. Humans have found ways to feed and clothe the hungry, although some greedy "middle men" would rather sell the donated food and clothing to enrich themselves rather than to feed and clothe those who are truly in need. We have invented more efficient and effective ways to communicate, and to travel faster and more safely. Technology to improve our lives and health evolves each day.

Through these improvements, our loving God is inspiring humans to make life on our planet Earth more just and merciful, more healthy and productive, and more forward looking and hopeful. In this sense, at least, we may agree with Teilhard and struggle against sickness and minimize even the ordinary diminishments that threaten us because it is "unquestionably the first act of our Father who is in heaven." And God wants us to help God to take "this cup" of suffering from us.

Spiritual Practices for Stage 1

In the following spiritual practices that flow from the guiding principles, Teilhard suggests what we can do and how we can act. He advises, "*Avoid any diminishments you see coming; get out of their way, if possible.*" Here are some spiritual practices that may be helpful.

The Fundamental Choice for Health

The foundational practice for stage 1 and all the other stages is the following fundamental choice:

I choose to live this day as healthily as possible in body, mind, and spirit.

33

This choice, or self-promise, is to be made daily. It is called a fundamental choice because it is the foundation of personal health. Without it, and the consciousness it brings to your life, it is quite easy to make poor health choices, even consciously, and excuse yourself.

Notice that this fundamental choice is worded so that, even if you were in the last days of a terminal illness, you could still make this choice and live by it.

Reflective Moment: Self-Help

Since stage 1 is primarily about avoiding actions that might harm your health, you might use this fundamental choice for health to ask yourself the following:

- *What are one or two things I might do or not do today to avoid inviting harm to my body or my physical well-being?*
- *What are one or two things I might do or not do today to avoid diminishment to my emotional, intellectual, or spiritual life?*

Reflective Moment: Self-Harm

If the previous exercise feels difficult to perform, try the following:

- *What are some things I typically do or don't do that may, perhaps in the long run, tend to harm my physical health or weaken me?*
- *What are some things I typically do or don't do that may, perhaps in the long run, tend to harm my psychological health, my self-esteem, or weaken my spirit?*

Using Your Imagination

One of the best ways for those who are suffering to get into resonance or coherence with the loving mind of God is to use sensory imagination. Rather than focusing on your illness and pain, picture an image of wellness. Visualize yourself whole and complete, doing all the positive and joyful things you would like to be doing. It could be singing, dancing, playing, running, or doing something you really enjoy or used to enjoy, alone or with others. Keep picturing yourself as healthy and fully alive.

Use all of your senses—sight, hearing, touch, taste, smell—to create such joyful events in your imagination as well as the pleasant emotions you felt at that time.

For some people, doing this imagining will take some practice, but the practice pays off. You can balance any fear, anger, and disharmony in your emotions by focusing on something that brings you joy. As you use your visualization in this positive way, you will begin to smile and feel an inner joy start to arise. It is this inner joy that helps raise your consciousness toward a resonance with God's love. Positive thoughts allow any healing energies available to you to enhance your healing.

Helping Yourself and Others

Teilhard reminds us that we are not the only focus of God's healing graces; there are many others who suffer too. He very clearly asserts, *We are all expected to help God remove diminishments from others.*

Teilhard also notes that it may help your own resolve to keep resisting if you recognize someone else being—or about to be—diminished and you choose to help others avoid their diminishment. Consider prayerfully the following:

- *Name one or two people being diminished that you might help.*
- *What specifically could you do for each of them?*
- *What cause might you support in your community, say, to help the hungry or the homeless?*

Prayer Forms for Stage 1

I Choose to Care

Teilhard reminds you that as long as human resistance is possible, the total Body of Christ will be resisting it too. Here, at stage 1, you might use the following, prayerfully reflecting on each statement:

- *I choose with all my heart to be healthy and to care for my health.*
- *I summon all the agents of my body—and within my body—to engage in their healing work.*
- *I imagine as clearly as I can the gradual and complete restoration of any parts of my body and mind that are weak or sick.*
- *I imagine warm and loving divine light showering my body.*
- *I remember that God wills the blossoming of Earth.*
- *I remember that God is within me, providing me with the energy I need.*

Thanking Your Body

Your body and mind are wonderful instruments. They are caring for your health and healing at every moment. There are literally millions of actions being performed throughout your body at each moment, of which you are unaware, that help keep you functioning, even when you are sick or in danger—perhaps especially at such times. All the organs and systems of your body want your health and are working harder than ever to keep you healthy. The appropriate response to the efforts of your body is thanksgiving and blessing.

As you know, your *genome* provides an analysis of your own genetic makeup. It identifies all the cells in your body that are uniquely yours, those that possess your unique DNA. However, many cells in your body do not share your DNA. Those non-you parts of you are called your *microbiome*.

A microbiome provides an analysis of the microbes that live on and in your body. Incidentally, these microbes outnumber the cells that have your own DNA by a factor of ten to one. They also account for more than half of your body weight. Like a living motel, on any given day, your body hosts thousands of different species of these microbes, each with its own DNA. They mate, multiply, interact, and fulfill their purposes inside you.

Many of these little creatures play important roles in our lives. For example, they regulate the energy we get from our food, they help us get rid of harmful entities inside our bodies as well as on our skin, and they help keep our immune system healthy. They also play a role in the evolution of new microbe species within us—and possibly influence our own human evolution. So, it is important to be grateful to our microbiome, for without all these very tiny beings working inside us, we could never maintain our health or fight oncoming bacterial or viral infections and other diseases.

During your expression of thanks to your body each morning and evening, affirm it, tell it that you know that it and all the creatures in it are working hard for your health, and that you will do all you can to assist that work. Formulate your gratitude in your own words.

Blessing Your Medications

Many people suffering from a physical or mental illness have been prescribed medications. One very simple way of cooperating with your healing is to bless your meds, as well as your other vitamins and supplements, before taking them.

In this simple prayer form, you are asked to hold in your hand any medication you are about to take and bless it with your love. You may also bless it with the ability to do only and very effectively the healing work for which it was prescribed, and that any unwanted side effects be removed or prevented from happening.[4]

Hold them in your hand or hold your hands over them in blessing, and say a prayer over them in your own words, or something like the following:

I bless you. I welcome you into my body. May you help my body to heal and may you do me no harm.

Or,

God, bless my medication. Grant that it may help my healing and do no harm.

You may use these blessing prayers whenever and as long as you are taking medication at all stages of your suffering.

In blessing your medication—or any other object that is meant to help in your healing or relief from a diminishment—you are engaging in this process with the clearest and most healthy intentions. Your intention and attention ensure that you are in the right frame of mind to take the medication and that the medication has its best chance of doing what it was intended to do for you.

As a variation on this blessing prayer, you may also invoke the blessing of God or of any other spiritual person whom you know would happily bless any medications you take or any healing process you engage in.

Maryann, who happens to be a Catholic, blesses her medications by making the Sign of the Cross over them before she consumes them.

Mantras

To strengthen your resolve to get past this diminishment, you may choose to make a mantra from one or more of Teilhard's suggestions at this stage:

- *I believe that God wants to free me from this diminishment.*
- *I detest this diminishment and will do everything in my power to be rid of it.*
- *I believe that God hates and rejects this diminishment as much as—or more than—I do.*
- *I know that God wants my help in removing this diminishment from me.*

Prayer before Medical Tests

A prayer before medical tests (or surgery or any other physical or mental "tests") can help you to remain at peace when you might need it most: in a time of great uncertainty when you might otherwise be tempted to see only darkness or failure around you. Remember that anxiety can feed on itself. When scheduling a procedure for ourselves or others, we wonder, "What will the outcome be? How will this affect my family or friends?" Those who live alone may wonder, "How will I manage if this is serious?"

Here is a sample prayer:

> *Dear God, as my loved ones and I await the results*
> *of medical tests about my illness,*
> *we offer you the energy we expend in our anxiety*
> *for our good and your glory.*

Calm us, as we know our worries don't add wisdom
    but rather stress to this situation.
Enlighten us, through the power of your Spirit,
    to make wise decisions when we get the results.
In these fragile, painful moments,
    we turn to you for grace and strength.
Comfort us as we place all our concerns
    in your loving hands and as we say,
"Thy Will Be Done."

A Meditative Prayer for Stage 1

I acknowledge that staying healthy
    is a lifelong challenge.
I know that You, Loving Mystery,
do not wish this diminishment to be happening.
I recognize that you respect the laws
    of nature and of evolution,
and that you grieve more than I do over this
    diminishment.
I realize that, in this diminishment,
    I join countless others who suffer.
I have difficulty accepting this loss of control,
and yet, I understand that this is a painful lesson
    I need to learn:
    my life is not about me,
    but about you in me,
    about me in the Universe.
May I learn to situate this diminishment
    within the far broader picture
    of life and death in evolution,
in which every component of this web
    of existence
    lives, grows, diminishes, and dies
    so that newness can arise.

Stage 2

Inner Resistance

*Even if you are starting to live under the diminishment
and it may defeat you, still resist it inwardly.*

❄

John was trying to avoid the flu, but he finally caught it.

*Donna was hiding, trying to avoid undeserved physical abuse
from her mother, but her mother finally found her and began
hitting her.*

*Phil was hoping the interview would go well, but the interviewer
told him he was not the person for this job, and Phil's inabil-
ity to land this job reinforced his sense of loss and of failing his
family.*

Isabel received divorce papers from her husband this morning.

*Betty was hoping that, because she had been faithful to the
chemotherapy and radiation, the biopsy would come back clear,
but the test proved positive for malignant cancer cells.*

In each case, a shift happened. The person went from trying to avoid
the diminishment to discovering that it was already happening. This
is a stage that focuses on the onset of a sickness or diminishment.
What does one do at this stage?

Even though you can no longer avoid or deny the diminishment, Teilhard recommends that you still resist it—at least inwardly.

The most powerful resistance to any enemy is an interior attitude, a commitment to do whatever you can or behave in any way
to resist. In wartime, if a soldier is captured and becomes a prisoner of
war, resistance is primarily an inner stance or attitude—not to cooperate with the enemy, not to give the enemy any information they
can use against you. In a similar way, at this stage of a diminishment,

do not give in to or even cooperate with the diminishment causing your suffering.

Your effort at this second stage builds an inward focus on your attitudes and beliefs, and calls for courage and determination. You may always, whether healthy or sick, recite and affirm daily the fundamental choice that you learned in stage 1:

> *I choose to live this day as healthily as possible in body, mind, and spirit.*

However, this affirmation acquires a different meaning at each stage of suffering. At this second stage, if your diminishment is a physical disease, you probably have already been diagnosed by your physician. If your suffering is a form of emotional or social diminishment, you have probably acknowledged the fact. For example, you have come to realize you are homosexual and will probably be treated by many others at work with prejudice. Suppose you have been sentenced to a period of time in prison for a crime, perhaps rightfully or unrightfully. The fact is you are in prison. In each above situation, the fundamental choice takes on a unique meaning.

At this stage, when the suffering is seen as being caused by some force beyond your control, the appropriate attitude toward it is resistance.

There are many different ways of displaying resistance. For example, suppose you are trying to avoid the flu or some other contagious disease, but it finally catches you. Don't deny that you have the illness or the diminishment. That would be deceiving yourself. Nevertheless, for as long as possible keep resisting it, confronting it, and fighting it. Don't give up in defeat immediately. Don't surrender. Taking meds and getting rest is a physical way of resistance. Sometimes, certain suffering is best resisted or fought with sleep and rest. If so, sleep may be the way to show your resistance. However, there are also ways of inner resistance.

Teilhard wants to make sure that when you resist the source of the diminishment interiorly, you do so without bitterness, resentment, or revolt.

You might take a hint from the approach of St. Catherine Labouré:

Whenever I go to the chapel, I put myself in the presence of our good Lord, and I say to him, "Lord I am here. Tell me what you would have me to do." If he gives me some task, I am content and I thank him. If he gives me nothing, I still thank him since I do not deserve to receive anything more than that. And then, I tell God everything that is in my heart. I tell him about my pains and joys, and then I listen….If you listen, God will also speak to you, for with the good Lord, you have to both speak and listen. God always speaks to you when you approach him plainly and simply.

Teilhard wants you not to forget that you have a unique purpose for your life on Earth, that you are expected to make a positive difference with your life. He reminds you that God wants you to be able—*physically*, *emotionally*, and *financially*—to contribute your part to the God project.

If you can still work and at least carry out some of your daily duties, Teilhard recommends it. If you cannot work physically, you may be able to contribute emotionally and intellectually with your prayer, your enthusiasm, your hopefulness, your wisdom, your experience, your compassion, and your sense of humor. If you happen to be relatively financially secure, you may be able to help certain worthwhile projects with your generosity.

Teilhard offers four guiding principles for this stage of inner resistance.

Guiding Principles

1. God Hates This Diminishment and Wants to Free You from It.

In Teilhard's essay, he observed, "Illness, by its very nature, tends to give those who suffer from it the impression that they are of no use, or even that they are a burden on the face of the earth."[1] People who are seriously ill are bound to feel that this diminishment has come upon them through no intention of their own—that, without choosing it, they have been tossed out of the mainstream of life, set apart from the activity going on all around them, and doomed to inaction. Teilhard wants to dispel these discouraging thoughts by showing them that there is a meaningful way to use their suffering in building the world. The usefulness of suffering energy is the most basic evolutionary truth Teilhard wants to communicate to those who suffer. Instead of feeling useless and a burden to society, those who suffer have a very constructive part to play in renewing the face of Earth.

2. Do Not Welcome Your Diminishments or Look Forward to Them.

"At the first approach of diminishments we cannot hope to find God except by loathing what is coming upon us and doing our best to avoid it," says Teilhard. "The more we repel suffering at that moment, with our whole heart and our whole strength, the more closely we cleave to the heart and action of God."[2]

3. Try to Forgive.

Forgiveness is essential to the healing process. Typically, we would like to identify the cause or sources of our affliction, and place our anger and blame on them. Nurturing anger or blame only keeps our focus on our affliction and away from our healing. Sometimes, the sources of our diminishments are outside of our control, as in an auto accident, a birth defect, the bite of a disease-carrying insect, a natural disaster, living in a theater of war, being born into a sick family, and so on. At other times, we can be the source of our own afflictions, as in driving an auto recklessly, not taking the normal protective precautions to avoid infection, inviting an angry response from others and causing division, and so on.

In each case, Teilhard recommends that we forgive the causes or sources of our suffering.

If we are the cause of our own sickness or loss, we learn to forgive ourselves, bless ourselves, and to reaffirm the fundamental choice to live healthily.[3]

If someone or something else is the cause of our suffering, we need to try to forgive them as well.

"As I walked out the door to the gate that would lead to my freedom," said Nelson Mandela, after twenty years behind bars, "I knew that if I didn't leave my bitterness and hatred behind, I'd still be in prison."

4. Accept the Diminishment.

In many cases, despite your inner and outer efforts to resist the illness or diminishment, the suffering is not going to retreat, go away, or disappear. Teilhard recommends that you keep resisting as long as resistance is possible, but in the back of your heart and mind let the thought be there that you may have to accept your illness or loss, that you may have lost this battle.

Spiritual Practices for Stage 2

As the foundation of your spiritual practices at this stage of your suffering, Teilhard reminds you that God hates and rejects this diminishment as much as—or more than—you do. Therefore, he encourages you to affirm the healing powers of your body and mind.

Kything

For Teilhard, when you are suffering, the entire Body of Christ suffers with you, just as when some illness or injury afflicts your body, your entire body suffers and all the various parts of your body coordinate their efforts to relieve the suffering or heal the injury. The same holds true in the Divine Milieu. All the members of Christ's Body want to help foster your healing, and during the earliest stages, they would join you in resisting your suffering or diminishment. Kything (rhymes with *tithing*) is a spiritual practice to help you become consciously aware of the other beings that are ready to cooperate in your healing process and growth in wholeness.

You may use this spiritual practice throughout all the stages of your suffering for comfort, consolation, companionship, courage, and clarity. We have put the practice here in this early stage where you can more easily learn to use it by kything with those who would help you in resisting or dealing with your diminishments.

Kything may be described as *the art of spirit-to-spirit connection.* We have ways of connecting with our bodies, through hugging and kissing. We have ways of communicating with our minds, through talking and writing. We also have ways of being spiritually connected, soul-to-soul, which we call *communion,* to distinguish it from verbal communicating. One of the ways of doing this spirit-to-spirit communion is kything. It is especially useful when your kything partner is not physically present—or has died. What is special about kything is that the person's spirit or soul is always available, since it is always alive in the Body of Christ and in the Divine Milieu.

Once you choose someone with whom you would like to connect, there are just five simple steps in the kything process:

1. *Grow quiet and centered.*
2. *Use your imagination to picture the person with whom you wish to kythe.*
3. *Use your imagination to picture a typical scene where you and the other person are (or were) connected, in a scene where you were happily together.*
4. *Say "Yes" to the image in step 3, that is, consciously picture the connection in your imagination into a present and real communion of spirits.*

Now that you are in a kythe, you are connected spirit-to-spirit. You may simply rest in this loving connection, or you can initiate a conversation. You may ask the other person for help in your healing or in coping with your suffering. You may stay connected with them as long as you wish.

5. *When you wish to end the kythe, thank your partner, bless them, and ask for a blessing for yourself.*

You may begin kything by connecting with someone you love—someone whom you know that would like to be lovingly present to you. Kything partners may be physically present or absent. They may be living or may have passed on. We are all living in the Divine Milieu, including angels and saints.

When you are in great pain and are physically alone, it is a good time to be in communion with someone you love who would want your healing. You may even gather a group of loving and caring people to kythe with you, all at the same time.

Before an operation, you may kythe with your surgeon, the nurses, and others who will take care of you during and after surgery, asking God to bless them and to guide the work of their hands.

If a healing procedure has been successful, you may reconnect in kythe with people who carried out the procedure as well as those who supported you, and bless them and say thanks.

Also, when you feel discouraged or disheartened, you may kythe with someone who would support you, affirm you, or make you laugh.

Laughter Medicine

Laughter has been shown to be a powerful medicine for mind and body. It can strengthen your immune system, lower pain, reduce stress, and help bring your body and mind back into balance. Humor and laughter have great healing qualities: they work fast, are fun, free, and easy to use.

Specifically, laughter relieves physical tension, decreases stress hormones, builds up infection-fighting immune cells, triggers the release of endorphins that create a sense of well-being, and protects your heart by increasing blood flow through your system. When you are laughing, it's almost impossible to feel anxious, angry, or sad.

There are many sources of humor. Choose the ones that are readily available to you and use them as healers.

- *Watch a funny movie or comedy shows on television.*
- *Read the newspaper's comic pages.*
- *Read books that collect comic strips or "best" cartoons.*
- *Check out Web sites devoted to humor, for example, Comedy Warriors.*
- *Spend time with people who love to laugh.*
- *Hang around young children.*
- *Play with a pet.*
- *Do something silly, anything to evoke laughter.*

Over thirty years ago, writer–editor Norman Cousins believed that a positive attitude, as well as belly laughs from watching slapstick films of the Marx Brothers in his sickbed, would help him contradict doctors' predictions of an early death from a rare ailment. Cousins won the gamble. He went on to live a long life and to write a book about the healing power of humor.

Prayer Forms for Stage 2

You are encouraged to use any and all of the spiritual practices or prayer forms that were introduced in stage 1, as well as the Universal Spiritual Practice noted on page 24.

Affirmation Prayer

In war, military personnel captured by an enemy force are trained to use a form of affirmation to maintain their resistance. They may recite frequently the Pledge of Allegiance or a familiar prayer. They may invent and repeat short statements to maintain their inner attitude, such as, "Thy will be done," or, "I know that God wants my release as much as I do," or, "Have mercy on me."

If you are still choosing to view your diminishment as an enemy who may be close to capturing you, you may use a form of affirmation prayer. Simply formulate your own affirmation statements.

Visualization Prayer

Again, military personnel captured by an enemy force often use forms of visualization to maintain their resistance. For example, they may visualize members of their family back home and choose to focus on that loving, caring image to maintain their resistance. Some may picture their nation's flag or the emblem of their service branch; others may think of their comrades who are still in harm's way and promise interiorly to remain silent in an effort to protect them.

Using these examples, what kinds of visualizations of people you love and care for can you use that would help you maintain your resistance? You can picture them in your imagination, and you may kythe with them.

Imagination Prayer

Teilhard encourages you not to give up at this early stage, but rather to resist being defeated by your diminishment, whatever it may be. Use your imagination to picture yourself in excellent health or, if not dealing with an illness, picture yourself living what you would envision as a normal, healthy life. Here are the simple steps, using your imagination:

1. *Become aware of God's presence all around you, giving life to everything you see—your bed, your chair, the lights, the clock, the sounds—everything in the room. See yourself living in a Divine Milieu.*
2. *Picture yourself as you were before you became ill (or diminished), doing the things you would normally do in an ordinary day—at home, your workplace or school, with family or friends. Spend some time on this step. Enjoy it!*
3. *Picture one typical enjoyable scene in great detail as vividly as you can with your imagination's eyes, ears, and touch. See the colors, shapes, and movements of people and things. Hear the sounds and voices you can recall hearing; identify each of them by name. In your imagination, touch familiar objects and let yourself handle and use them as you usually would.*
4. *While imagining yourself acting, speaking, and feeling full of life, tell God, "I choose this. I choose what I am picturing. I choose to live life as fully as I can, and as long as I can be an instrument of your work, compassion, love, and joy in the world. I choose it provided it will help renew the face of Earth."*

You may repeat this exercise twice a day—or even more often—using different scenes from your "healthy" life.

If the diminishment you are struggling against is something other than a physical or mental illness, you may modify step 2 accordingly. In your imagination, picture yourself living, acting, and feeling free of this diminishment. The rest of the steps remain the same.

For example, Cathy's suffering is her discouragement at not being able to find a job after weeks of searching and applying. In step 2, she envisioned in her imagination working in a job she would enjoy that used all of her talents. In her imagery, she included a picture of her preferred workplace location, feeling the support and friendship of her coworkers, being assigned a work schedule she liked, leaving the workplace feeling happy and content at the end of the day.

As another example, Sue's diminishment is living in an abusive home, where she has been verbally and physically abused since she was of school age. In step 2, Sue imagined herself living in her own apartment and sharing it with a close friend. She would picture the apartment, where it is located, what the apartment windows look out on, how it would be decorated, and the close friend who would be sharing the place with her.

There are many other uses for the imagination prayer, for example, before surgery picture yourself enjoying an optimally successful outcome.

Before surgery, Jill, using her imagination, pictured herself back in her hospital bed after surgery with the doctor coming to her and telling her that the surgery had been very successful. It was everything she and the physician had hoped for. She also imagined herself healing rapidly and fully with no problems or complications.

The imagination prayer may be used before any major step, transition, or procedure in your sickness or diminishment, to envision the process outcome in a most positive way.

A Meditative Prayer for Stage 2

*I believe that the Divine Energy flowing through
all things
wishes that all things blossom.
I believe that You wish me to blossom.
I accept reluctantly that illness, disease, old age,
disability,
may be impairing this.
I am not giving up or giving in.
I am trying to accept the "new normal" for myself.
May I have the courage and the trust to accept it.
May I continue to believe that You wish for
my health,*

and that I have a purpose to fulfill for You
in my life.
May I continue to believe that in the end,
all shall be well
and all manner of things shall be well.
Through my pain, may I continue to experience
Your loving Presence.

Part Two

STAGES OF
TRANSFORMATION

Stages 3, 4, and 5 introduce a new approach to and perspective on suffering.[1] In some ways, these stages of transformation best reflect the originality of Teilhard's approach to suffering.

The first stage of transformation, stage 3, is focused on *prayer*, which helps a person make two shifts in thinking.

The first shift takes you away from your previous exclusive focus on a cure and brings you to a desire for healing and wholeness. Here, Teilhard acknowledges that you may still be wishing for and seeking a cure for your disease, illness, or diminishment. In fact, it is natural and very understandable for a person, at any stage, not to want to give up all hope of a cure.

The second shift calls for spiritual activities and prayers that help take you away from seeing your diminishment as an enemy or an opponent, and toward seeing it as a resource with powerful meaning and significance. The reason for the emphasis on prayer in stage 3 is to facilitate these two initial transformations.

In stage 4, Teilhard acknowledges that *patience* is needed in learning to live in this transformed state, where hopefully you will begin, normally and automatically, to see your pain and suffering as a positive and powerful resource in helping achieve God's plan for Earth.

In stage 5, which focuses on *choice*, you begin to realize that there are many ways to apply the energy released in your suffering.

This very practical chapter presents some of the laws that govern the use and usefulness of energy generated in unavoidable suffering.

When you were in full strength, you were able to direct your activities and energy toward a specific goal—finish this project, organize that event, raise this child, teach that class, resolve this conflict, and so on. Now that you are unquestionably ill or diminished, you must begin to look at your physical life in a different way.

This diminishment may have also affected your emotional and spiritual life. For example, whereas before your illness or diminishment you may have felt hopeful, now you may feel discouraged; before you may have felt confident and successful, now you may tend to feel frustrated and angry much of the time; before you may have felt useful when people came to you for help and support, and now you must begin to accept the fact that you will be mostly on the receiving end. Watching others going on with their normal busy lives, you may feel envious and jealous; before you may have felt free to go and do whatever you wanted, whereas now you may feel helpless and constrained.

While it used to feel easy and natural to pray and thank God for your blessings, now you may find it hard to feel comfort in prayer; instead of blessings, you may feel that God has placed on you an unwelcome burden. Before, when Jesus said, "Take my yoke," you could easily welcome it; now you don't find it at all "easy and light," as Jesus had promised.

During these middle stages of suffering, you will need to learn how to make friends with unwanted emotions like fear, anxiety, discouragement, frustration, and anger. Such emotions were probably never felt this strongly during earlier stages, when you were actively fighting and resisting your diminishment, but now they seem to be taking center stage inside you.

Remember, in any evolutionary spirituality there are two functions: first, your personal spiritual growth in consciousness and compassion; and second, the collective spiritual growth of all your brothers and sisters on the planet, who are participants and coworkers with you in God's great evolutionary project of transformation.

So we need to introduce new guiding principles, new spiritual activities, and prayer forms that help cope with these unwelcome and apparently unhelpful feelings. Actually, as you will discover, these activities and prayers can be useful in a number of ways.

A New Focus

These stages of transformation mark a different approach or relationship to pain and suffering. During the first two stages, the focus was on avoiding and resisting pain and suffering—any disease, illness, or other diminishments—with both inner and outer resistance. Hopefully, the primary aim or purpose was to achieve the cure of an illness or removal of a diminishment, especially the pain and suffering it might have brought with it.

However, if the illness or diminishment could not be avoided or cured, despite all your inner and outer resistance, you enter stage 3—the first stage of transformation. Here, the sufferer acknowledges that a cure has not occurred, that the illness or diminishment still has to be dealt with, and that the need now is to focus your healing and wholeness.

This new focus requires a new mindset, a transformation of thinking, and two shifts in your purpose and objectives.

The First Shift

In this first shift, your objective or purpose changes from seeking a *cure* to seeking *healing*.

There is an important difference between getting cured and being healed. *Getting cured* means you no longer have the disease, illness, or diminishment that was threatening you. The problem has disappeared. It has departed; it is no longer present. You do not have to deal with it anymore.

In contrast, *being healed* means to be made whole. Wholeness means to feel fully alive and present to life, capable of expressing joy, humor, gratitude, forgiveness, compassion, generosity, and love—all the things a healthy and whole person can feel and do, *even though you are still experiencing unavoidable pain and suffering.*

Sometimes healing includes getting cured from an illness or disease; but only sometimes. More importantly, you can be *healed* even if the illness or disease is still present in your life and there is no hope for a *cure*.

Being healed means that you have learned to live a healthy and whole life despite your sickness or diminishment. You are at peace, even though you are still ill. The diminishment is still part of your daily reality, but you have learned to cope with it and still live a happy and relatively full life. In an extreme case, you may be dying in the final stage of cancer, yet you feel like a whole human being. Though not cured of your illness, you have been healed. You can live each day with a sense of peace, a purpose for being where you are at this moment. Being healed means you still feel that you can contribute to the work of building the kingdom of God on Earth. Your suffering energy is still needed for renewing the face of the Earth.

The distinction between getting cured and being healed is centrally important in relation to these middle stages of suffering. During the earlier stages, your primary efforts were typically directed toward a cure—the avoidance or removal of your illness, disease, or diminishment. In all the further stages of suffering, your primary purpose changes. Instead of seeking a cure, it shifts to working toward your own healing and wholeness—and that of others, of course.

The Second Shift

Along with the shift from curing to healing comes the question of what to do with all the energy you expend on the unavoidable pain and suffering that accompany this illness or diminishment. This shift requires another change in the way you think about your pain and suffering.

In this shift, you learn to give a new identity to your pain and suffering, and you develop a new way of relating to it. In the earlier stages, you may have viewed your illness or diminishment as a kind of opponent or adversary that must be conquered and destroyed; in this shift, your suffering now becomes your ally and a major resource in fostering your spiritual growth. Before, if you treated an oncoming illness as your enemy, now, you learn to treat it as a colleague or partner. Before, even if with God's help and approval you resisted your illness or diminishment, and the limitations it brought with it, in the earlier stages, now, the pain and suffering from that same diminishment become something you accept and embrace. You embrace the suffering because it becomes for you a tool for spiritual growth for yourself and others. It becomes a source or structure for transformation—a transformation that is not only personal but also has its effects on collective humanity.

Prayer

*While continuing to struggle against your unwelcome
diminishments, recognize that they can become for you a loving
principle of transformation through prayer.*

❂

During the first two stages, your focus was on avoiding and resisting
oncoming diminishments with both inner and outer resistance, where
Teilhard asked you to treat your suffering as an opponent or enemy.

In stage 3, since the pain and suffering are not going away but
will unavoidably remain with you, Teilhard asks you to approach and
consider your suffering in new ways by developing a new mindset
toward it. The new mindset calls for two shifts in the way you think
about your suffering and relate to it.

In the first shift, you now begin seeking healing and wholeness,
that is, finding ways to live as fully as you can while enduring your
suffering.

In the second shift, with your enduring pain and suffering,
Teilhard asks you to begin thinking about your pain and suffering as
friends or partners in helping you renew the face of the Earth.

Those two changes will require *prayer* (stage 3), *patience* (stage
4), and important *choices* (stage 5). During these stages of transformation, you will begin to accept and embrace your suffering because it
becomes a tool of spiritual growth for yourself and others.

The following prayer begins to express these mindset shifts:

A Meditative Prayer for Stage 3

*I am aware of the hostile forces working
against my growth and blossoming.
I recognize that, in some way, these hostile forces are also of You,*

and that, in ways I don't understand,
this is also You working in me.
At least, may I see that whatever is happening
to me
is happening in Your Divine Milieu,
that You are the Space in which my life of pain
is unfolding.
May I come to see that I am not alone in
my affliction.
In my pain, I am in good company:
in the company of millions around the world
who are ill and dying at this moment
or are hurting in many other ways.
May I become aware that, even in my suffering,
and through my prayer,
I can be a blessing to others,
if only by the way I bear it.
May I come to accept
that my pain marks some form of transition
to a different form of being myself.

Guiding Principles

1. There Are Bound to Be Conflicts, Competition, Loss, and Failure.

The challenge in these transformational stages is to acknowledge and remember that your diminishments and unwelcome experiences are happening in the Divine Milieu. Moreover, Teilhard wants you to remember that the Divine Milieu itself is also in process, also subject to the laws of evolution, and also still incomplete.

All creatures on Earth are struggling for their fulfillment. Some are doing it in healthy ways, others in less healthy ways. However, because there are so many creatures struggling all in the same place and at the same time for their own fulfillment, it is inevitable that conflicts, confrontations, loss, failure, confusion, disappointment, rejection, abandonment, accidents, sickness, death, and other forms of evil will occur. All of these unwelcome experiences tend to generate a thousand variations of pain and suffering. They delay and detour our path to self-fulfillment. This is reality. These are the facts of evolutionary life.

God, who created this gradually evolving universe, cannot simplify complexity, eliminate confusion, prevent losses, remove all sickness, correct all mistakes, cancel all debts, deny free will, control every moment of your life, or do away with death. These are all unavoidable parts of the evolutionary process happening in the Divine Milieu.

Our life in process was well described in a statement by Martin Luther. He wrote,

> This life is not justice,
> But growth in justice,
> Not health but healing,
> Not being but becoming,
> Not rest but exercise.
> We are not yet what we shall be,
> But we are growing toward it.
> The process is not yet finished,
> But it is going on.
> This is not the end,
> But it is the road.
> All does not yet gleam in glory,
> But all is being purified.

2. Diminishments Can Promote the Law of Attraction-Connection-Complexity-Consciousness.

When we contract an illness, suffer an accident, get laid off from a job, or divorce from a marriage, it brings more complexity into our lives. Painful situations like these, unavoidable as they often are, connect us with people we may never have met before. They create new connections and relationships. They require new awareness and new ways of behaving. Things happening as a result of a disease or diminishment challenge us to use the Law of Attraction-Connection-

Complexity-Consciousness, in other words, to promote the evolutionary process.

As John Henry Cardinal Newman observed, "God has created me to do Him some definite service...therefore I will trust Him....If I am in sickness, my sickness may serve Him....He knows what He is about."[1]

Teilhard says that when we are healthy, we are connected with God's work in the world through our personal growth and daily active efforts to make a difference. However, in times of illness or pain, when we cannot perform our daily jobs, we discover there is a complementary way of communion with God and cooperating with God's work in the world. In this complementary way, our way of making a difference shifts. It can no longer be through self-development and self-expression in our daily workday efforts, but by making a positive difference with our suffering energy.

Spiritual Practices for Stage 3

In chapter 2, you learned to use the Universal Spiritual Practice as a useful activity whenever and wherever suffering occurred. It showed you how to redirect the energy generated by your pain and suffering.

From this stage onward, it will become perhaps the most important and powerful spiritual activity you will perform daily—even hourly, especially when your pain is most intense. Your suffering energy has become the primary force available to you at this moment for transforming the world. As we move forward, use this spiritual practice as frequently as possible.

List Your Unwelcome Feelings

In attempting to make the difficult mental and emotional shift from seeking a cure to seeking healing and wholeness, you are bound to feel resistance to this shift. Each person will experience different forms of emotional resistance—anger, denial, fear, frustration, helplessness, and so on.

In this spiritual practice, you are asked to make a list of those unwelcome feelings that are most prominent. Making a list is important for two reasons. First, the physical act of writing down the names of these negative feelings makes you conscious that you are experiencing feelings that you might not want to acknowledge. Once they are there on your list, you can't deny them. Second, you now have in your hand a list of unwelcome feelings that you will want to dialogue with and discover the wisdom each one has to teach you.

Dialogue with an Unwelcome Feeling

Just as a good musician, because of an audience's preferences, must learn to perform songs he or she may not like as well as other more personal favorites, so in these stages of transformation you must acknowledge unwelcome feelings and accept the fact that you are capable of feeling and expressing frustration, anger, loss, jealousy, and the like.

When an unwelcome feeling arises and captures your attention, Teilhard suggests you greet it as a friend, companion, or teacher. As a wise man once observed, "I have never met a person who could not teach me something I did not know."

Give the unwelcome feeling a name: "Hello, Anger! How do you do?" "Hi, Frustration, come here and talk to me." "Greetings, Loneliness, perhaps you have some wisdom to teach me."

You are encouraged to have individual conversations with each of these difficult feelings as they emerge. The idea is to be mindful of them; to recognize, identify, and name them as they arise; and to welcome them as companions or teachers on your journey toward wholeness and holiness.

Here's one way to do it: Picture the unwelcome feeling that you chose to talk to. Give the feeling a shape, a voice, and a personality so that you can dialogue with it. And very naturally in your imagination, as if the feeling character were in the room with you, carry on a conversation. As you picture the unwelcome character sitting or standing nearby, ask a question (by writing it down) and welcome any response that surfaces within you. Write down whatever response you hear inside you.

Here are some sample questions to open and close a dialogue with an unwelcome feeling:

- *Why did you step into my life today?*
- *What did you come to teach me?*
- *What do I need to learn from you to help me cope with my situation?*
- *Have I met you before? When?*
- *Have you come into my life often and I have been unaware of you?*
- *Do you have a gift for me?*
- *Do you want something from me?*

At the end of your dialogues, you may say thank you for the conversation and for what you learned from it. Then, say good-bye or invite the feeling character to come back again, suggesting that you may have more to learn from it.

Even though you are diminished, if you still have the ability to write down on paper the contents of your dialogue with an unwelcome visitor, please do it, as it will make this activity much more powerful.

Dialogues with difficult and unwelcome feelings that arise are important to help clear the way for a more direct form of divine contact and engagement.

SAMPLE DIALOGUE WITH FEAR

Fear is often at the root of many unwelcome emotions; they mask the other unwelcome feelings because fear usually renders people helpless. Fear tends to swallow up energy, courage, determination, and a sense of hope. Angela is often overcome by fear, especially lying in bed at night. Her heart condition has been getting worse instead of getting better. Here is a dialogue she reported with her Fear:

Angela (A): Hello Fear. You're here again preventing me from sleeping. During the day, I noticed you brought some of your buddies, none of whom I really like—anxiety, worry, suspicion.

Fear (F): You should have a conversation with each of them sometime. They have a lot to teach you.

A: No thanks! Please disinvite them! Ask them to leave me alone. It took enough courage to get myself to talk to you. You are scary enough.

F: But I am the gateway to your freedom and your growth as a person.

A: How do you figure that?

F: Now that you are actually talking to me, I can help you. First of all, start by telling me one of the things you are afraid of.

A: I'm afraid of lots of things in this hospital, for instance, picking up infections that are floating around in the air, or a nurse accidentally giving me a wrong medication, or lab reports coming back with bad news, or how to pay for all the expenses that are mounting up here in the hospital.

F: Okay, okay, enough! Those are legitimate worries. But, come on, tell me what you *really* fear.

A: What do you mean?

F: Underneath all those reasonable fears you just listed, there are more serious ones.

A: Do you want to know what I fear deep down?

F: Of course. That's why I'm here talking with you.

A: I'm afraid with my illness that my husband won't really want to love me anymore.

F: There! You've said it.

A: So, what do I do with this fear?

F: Nothing. You've already done it. You've released it. Before you released it, it was hindering your healing. That fear was generating all kinds of negative chemicals into your system. Now that you've released that fear, the healthier parts of your immune system can go to do the work they were meant to do.

A: But it's still a fear.

F: Of course, but it is no longer a fear destroying you from the inside. If you really want to analyze it some more, you can now do it with a bit more objectivity, and consider how realistic that fear is.

Prayer Forms for Stage 3

With unwelcome thoughts and feelings that arise especially during the three stages of transformation, it may seem as though your heart's desire is no longer still connected to God's desire, and that you have been distracted from your life's purpose.

At these moments, in every stage of suffering, the challenge is to reconnect to your life's purpose and the most effective use of your suffering energy. There are special kinds of prayer forms that will enable you to make whatever reconnection may be needed.

Many of our sacred traditions have discovered that gratitude is the best spiritual medicine to alleviate suffering. Thanksgiving is also an excellent prayer form to help you make the shift from treating your suffering and diminishments as enemies to embracing them as powerful sources of energy for helping God's work in the world. Paradoxical as it may seem, showing appreciation to God and others really works. Here are some prayer forms to get you started. You may spontaneously find others.

Thanksgiving in Time of Suffering and Loss

Thank you, God, for when I experience…
- *Failed intentions, I may renew my resolutions.*
- *Trouble, I can learn to deepen my trust in you.*
- *Sickness, I can show gratitude to all who care for me and the medications that help.*
- *Loss, I can value you more and appreciate what I have.*
- *Rejection, it gives me an opportunity to forgive.*
- *Pain, I have the chance to experience some little amount of what others experience so much of.*
- *Mistakes, I can practice forgiving myself.*
- *Tragedy, I can spread compassion and offer comfort to others.*
- *Being forgotten, I can reach out to others who are lonely.*

Gratitude for Things I Take for Granted

Using the list below or any other items you choose, reflect on the item selected, and begin to list the many things this item provides for you. As you consider each service it provides, say thanks to God for it. Also, send a blessing to those who help provide it. You can even thank the item itself.

Thank you, God, for what I take for granted:
- *Electricity*
- *Water*
- *Plumbing*
- *Furniture*
- *Phones*
- *Television*
- *Closets*
- *Automobiles*
- *Batteries*
- *Internet*
- *Pets*
- *Neighbors*
- *Family*

(You may add to this list.)

Terry began listing the things he enjoyed that depended on electricity. He stopped listing after finding twenty-five items in his home that were dependent on electricity. The next day he began a list of things outside his home that required electricity and that he counted on for his enjoyment and safety. He found another twenty items.

Gratitude for Parts of My Body

As in the previous prayer form, use the list below or any other body part or bodily function you choose, reflect on the part or function selected, and begin to list what it provides for you. As before, say thanks to God for it and thank the item itself.

Thank you, God, for those parts of my body that are still functioning for me:
- *Lungs*
- *Heart*
- *Kidneys*
- *Bladder*
- *Brain*

- *Stomach*
- *Circulation*
- *Immune system*
- *Memory*
- *Intelligence*
- *Sense of humor*

If, for example, you don't know what function your kidneys perform, google "kidneys." You may be surprised how important that part of your body is in keepng you healthy.

"Help Me to Remember" Prayer

O God, when I have food,
help me to remember the hungry.
When I have work,
help me to remember the jobless.
When I have a home,
help me to remember those who have no
    home at all.
When I am without pain,
help me to remember those who suffer,
and as I remember,
help me to destroy my complacency,
bestir my compassion,
to be concerned enough to help,
by word and deed,
those who cry out for what we take
    for granted.
Amen.

For Those Who See Suffering as a Waste

Pray for those persons who are suffering and who do *not* know how to redirect their suffering energy to good purpose. Kything is a most helpful tool to maximize the power of this prayer form.

Stage 4

Patience

*In patience, leave the time and manner of the transformation of
your diminishments to one greater than you, namely, to the
Holy Spirit that is directing God's project on Earth.*

❋

Following your new transformational mindset begun in stage 3,
Teilhard asks you, first, to continue to see your suffering and diminishments as your allies and, second, to find creative ways to use the
energy generated by your pain to promote God's project for Earth.
Completing these shifts requires patience. Learning to live with suffering takes patience.

Teilhard would agree with inspirational author Joyce Meyer,
who says, "Patience is not simply the ability to wait—it's how we
behave while we're waiting."[1] Teilhard might have expressed it as,
"Patience is not shown simply in our ability to endure suffering—
but in how we train ourselves to spend wisely the energy we generate in suffering."

Mary of Nazareth also offers some perspective on patience as
she lived out the months and years after the Annunciation. Notice
that she experiences much suffering as well as much joy.

"Let it be done to me according to your word" is how Mary
expressed her free choice to cooperate with God's will. It was her
version of the choice we all make in prayer each day when we say,
"Thy will be done on Earth." That expression from the Lord's Prayer
is both a collective prayer and a personal prayer. Collectively, we want
God's will to be accomplished this day all over the planet by governments, businesses, organizations, dioceses, congregations, and families. However, we also want God's will to be accomplished by us

personally, as individuals, for we too have things to do—or endure—this day that are part of God's will for us.

Mary had to reaffirm her choice daily; it became a fundamental choice for the rest of her life. For those who suffer, that same choice—"Thy will be done on Earth"—can also become a daily fundamental choice.

If we think of a young pregnant unmarried woman in a small village in Galilee, as Mary was, with all the talk and gossip she had to endure once her unwed pregnancy became noticeable, then we realize how important it was for her to reaffirm her choice each day: "Let it be done to me according to your word." As notice of her pregnancy spread throughout the village, and comments about her were made, her suffering would have grown more difficult and painful. She had to endure silently each taunt and each accusing glance from other men and women in the community.

For those who must endure emotional pain, which is sometimes harder to bear than physical pain, Mary offers us a way to direct the energy we spend in suffering toward productive ways for God's project.

The current slang expression, "Whatever!" usually spoken in a tone of resignation, is not really a formal choice like that of Mary, but rather a throwaway expression that discards and wastes the power of choice; it abandons the capacity to release and direct one's energy for a positive purpose.

Mary did not respond to the angel's invitation by saying simply, "Whatever!" That would have been to cast aside and waste powerful spiritual energy. However, in saying, "Let it be done to me according to your word," Mary aligns her choice and all the energy she would generate in enduring suffering with the will of God, and redirects it toward the healing and development of the world.

Like Mary, we can say, "Let it be done to me according to your word," not only on days when we must endure pain and suffering, but also on good days when nice things happen. For example, Mary was consoled and affirmed when Joseph came and claimed her for his wife, even though she was pregnant and shamed by the community. She could also reaffirm her choice joyfully, when her baby was safely delivered in Bethlehem; when shepherds came and adored the child; when wise men came and brought gifts; and when Mary and

Joseph brought him to be blessed in the temple where they encountered the priest, Simeon, and the prophetess, Anna.

Those who suffer may use Mary's words: "Let it be done to me according to your word." That choice holds for good days and bad days.

Guiding Principles

1. God Is Capable of Making Good Come Out of Evil.

One obvious way of bringing good from evil is in the lessons you learn through suffering or the qualities you develop such as patience and forgiveness.

In his book *Letters to a Young Poet*, Rainer Maria Rilke writes,

> I want to beg you, as much as I can, dear sir, to be patient toward all that is unresolved in your heart and to try to love the *questions themselves* like locked rooms and like books that are written in a very foreign tongue. Do not seek the answers, which cannot be given you because you would not be able to live them. And the point is, to live everything. *Live* the questions now. Perhaps you will then gradually, without noticing it, live along some distant day into the answer.[2]

As a reflective exercise, you might choose one of your own "unresolved questions," as Rilke suggests, one that seems to be "locked up" or "hidden." Try to love the question itself—embrace it, hold it lovingly—without searching for an answer. Try loving the question and living "into the answer."

Such unanswered questions might be the following: "Why did I get this illness?" "How will I function after this accident?" "What will happen to my children if I die?" Teilhard, knowing that he was forbidden to publish his writings, must have had to live with this unanswered question: "What will happen, after I die, to all the books and articles I have written for God's greater glory?"

2. Everything Is Capable of Being Transformed into Good.

This principle is easy to say but hard to believe, especially when you can't imagine how continued suffering or the agonizing pain of someone you love can ever be seen as something "capable of being transformed into good." Yet Teilhard asks you to keep affirming this principle of suffering until you can begin to imagine creative ways of transforming the suffering you endure. It is a tremendously creative act to move from seeing suffering as an enemy to seeing it as a friend, or to see the potential for good in something that appears so evil and unwelcome.

Spiritual writer Henri Nouwen adds another perspective on patience: "The word patience means the willingness to stay where we are and live the situation out to the full in the belief that something hidden there will manifest itself to us."[3]

No matter what poor choices you may have made up to now regarding your illness or diminishment, and no matter how self-destructive or destructive of others those choices might have been, Teilhard assures us that the situation is always somehow redeemable, perhaps not immediately, but in time.

3. The Transformation May Not Be Completed Instantly.

Everyone needs patience, but those who suffer usually need it the most. As St. Francis de Sales put it, "Have patience with all things, but first of all with yourself." Be gentle with yourself. Forgive those pessimistic thoughts telling you to give up trying to befriend suffering or to belittle your potential to contribute to God's work in the world.

Writer Anne Lamott suggests you train your wayward mind with kindness and patience as you would house-train a new pet. She writes, "Try looking at your mind as a wayward puppy that you are trying to paper train. You don't drop-kick a puppy into the neighbor's yard every time it piddles on the floor. You just keep bringing it back to the newspaper."[4]

The following prayer puts together these three guiding principles:

I am trying to understand that my diminishments
are somehow part of the greater scheme.
That what I experience as pain and evil may, in fact,
lead to something greater, somewhere,
even here.
May I develop the firm conviction
that, out of every situation,
no matter how dire,
You, the God of the Universe,
in an evolving universe,
can transform evil into good,
diminishment into blossoming.

Spiritual Practices for Stage 4

As a gentle reminder, please keep using those earlier spiritual practices and prayer forms that you found useful, such as kything. Also continue to use the Universal Spiritual Practice in redirecting the energy generated by your pain and suffering.

Of course, some of the earlier spiritual practices may need to be adapted to different stages of suffering.

Dialogue with an Unwelcome Feeling

You were introduced to this practice in stage 3, but it remains useful at all stages, since unwelcome feelings will undoubtedly continue to distract you. This practice shows how to make those feelings useful and profitable.

Here is a sample dialogue between Reggie and Impatience. Reggie is a cancer patient who is undergoing chemo and radiation therapy for the second time. He is usually a very busy businessman and has little tolerance for inefficiency and lateness. Unfortunately, the hospital where he goes for treatment is always running late. Impatience is rather an obsession with him, and while he has been focused on directing his suffering energy toward the success of his grandson's health, feelings of impatience with many aspects of his life continue to distract him. He decided to dialogue with Mr. Impatience. Here is a sample of his dialogue as he wrote it:

Reggie (R): Hello Mr. Impatience. You are an old familiar companion. I notice you hanging around a lot lately.

Impatience (I): But you normally don't talk to me. You feel my presence but don't acknowledge me.

R: To be honest, I'd rather you weren't around.

I: But I am part of your life, a rather important part.

R: Ha! You never give up, I'll grant you that. You've been around most of my life.

I: Why do you think I have been a part of your life for so long?

R: Are you preparing me for something important?

I: That's right! I have been working with you for years because you're going to need my services badly very soon. I'm really on your side. I'm one of the most faithful companions you have.

R: Well, you've always provided me with a sin to confess. "Bless me, Father, for I have sinned. I have been impatient many times."

I: You know, I wince every time you treat me as a sin. I am your friend.

R: So, tell me, how are you my friend?

I: I recognize that you sometimes misuse me, but it is often through me that you get access to your own sense of power and righteous anger. You have accomplished a lot for the kingdom of God through me. I push you to get things done, and to complete them in record time. I nudge you to use your impatience gently to push other people to get things done.

R: Well.

I: How often have you come into a large line of people waiting to be cared for, and while everyone else just stands around helplessly, you speak up and get extra help to come and care for everyone?

R: So, that's you at work in me?

I: Yes. I really am your friend and I help you to help others, or at least get help for them. I release a lot of your potential energy.

R: Thank you. I had no idea how you have been working in me.
I: All I ask is that you use me well.

Forgiveness

One of the spiritual practices that may take some patience is clearing your mind and spirit through forgiveness. Healing and wholeness remain incomplete as long as there is unforgiveness in your heart. Unforgiveness and all-embracing love are rather incompatible qualities. They do not sit well together.

The following exercise is one that you may want to repeat often:

- *Forgive yourself for any failures or lapses.*
- *Especially forgive anyone who has offended you.*
- *Clear your brain and memory of any hateful thoughts or wishes for revenge or getting even, and so forth.*

Spiritual Will Making

One of the things to do during these stages of transformation is to make out a spiritual will. Just as people make out a financial will, stating how they want their money and property to be passed on, in a similar way people who are suffering may find it a satisfying self-awareness experience to make out a spiritual will, outlining how they want what is important in their life to be passed on.

Your life is more than the money or possessions you accumulated, it is itself a testimony of what beliefs, attitudes, and values you want to be passed on. Here are some sample questions to help you make out your will:

- *How do you want your life and the way you lived to be continued and developed by those who follow after you?*
- *How do you want your life to be remembered and honored?*
- *Do you have any specific qualities you want bestowed on certain members of your family or others? Is there some specific quality, such as patience or generosity or a love for science, that you had begun to develop that you would want your children or grandchildren to develop further?*

If you are too sick to write such a spiritual will yourself, perhaps you can get someone to assist you. They may begin by asking you questions such as, "What values, attitudes, and beliefs would you like to pass on? What, for example, would you like to bequeath to your grandson, Luke? What would you like to bequeath to your granddaughter, Susan?"

Prayer Forms for Stage 4

Just because a certain prayer form may have been introduced at an earlier stage is no reason to stop doing it at a later stage. Use any earlier prayer forms that you still find valuable and supportive.

Thanksgiving in Time of Suffering

Any prayer for redirecting your pain or suffering energy in positive ways may begin with thanksgiving.

> *I thank you, God,*
> *that, with the energy of my suffering,*
> *I am able to cooperate with you and your Holy Spirit*
> *   in renewing the face of Earth.*
> *I want to help bring about an increase of peace, love,*
> *   and awareness among our human family,*
> *and I am grateful that you can use the energy of*
> *   my pain and suffering in positive ways*
> *to further that grand process you have begun.*

A Prayer of Gratitude

This is a prayer that every human can say:

> *Dear God, creator and sustainer of all things*
> *that have existed, exist now, and will come to be,*
> *many of your creations are inert like rocks,*
> *many like plants and flowers are pretty but never*
> *   get to move around,*
> *and animals are driven to act primarily out of instinct.*

As the story goes, you shaped us humans out of the
  mud of the earth.
Thankfully, you allowed me to become some of the mud
that got to
- *sit up and look around*
- *stand up and walk around*
- *explore and touch things*
- *run and play*
- *drink and eat*
- *dance and sing*
- *hold a puppy or a kitten*
- *laugh and cry*
- *tell stories and make them up*
- *make friends and share*
- *kiss and get hugged*
- *forgive and make up*
- *hope and plan.*
(Add as many as you like of your own endings.)

After you have finished your listing of things you were able to do in life, say a heartfelt thank you to God.

Alternative Prayer of Gratitude

If you are a caretaker of people confined to bed or a wheelchair, one of the most important things you can do is to help them remember the good things that happened in their lives. To do this, you might engage them in the previous prayer game each day.

Begin by reciting the opening lines of the prayer, as above, and invite your patient to respond, perhaps with some coaching or hinting on your part. Let them reply with words describing what they did or experienced during their lifetime. Encourage them to reach back in memory to all the persons, places, things, activities, and events for which they are grateful. Invite them to tell you stories associated with each different event.

As you practice this prayer game, your patient will become accustomed to finding more things to be grateful for. It is allowed and even encouraged to let them get warmed up each time you do it together by listing the same dozen things over and over.

When they seem to slow down, encourage them to explore their lives more deeply. You will then get very specific images—their first romantic kiss; the bite of an apple that they picked from a tree; getting their first iPhone; holding their firstborn five minutes after delivery; feeding the squirrel that used to come begging at the back door.

As patients recall these precious memories, don't be in a hurry to move on. Rather, invite the patient to go back into the special moment just mentioned, and relive it in imagination as fully as possible and recall in greater sensory detail the event and its surroundings.

Prayer to the Holy Spirit

This is a very traditional prayer found in any book of prayers. It expresses God's project very simply. It is a prayer that asks the Holy Spirit to recreate you and fire you up to be one who helps renew the face of the Earth.

> *Come, Holy Spirit, fill the hearts of your faithful.*
> *And kindle in them the fire of your love.*
> *Send forth your Spirit and they shall be created.*
> *And you will renew the face of the Earth.*

Prayer for Patience

Throughout the centuries, it has been said that Christ is closest to us in our suffering. This prayer for patience may help you cope during those times when you need to feel God's presence most.

> *Dear Lord,*
> *by allowing me to experience this pain,*
> *so that I may share in your suffering on the cross for the love*
>   *of all creation,*
> *you are taking a chance.*
> *You know that I might either draw closer to you for strength,*
> *or turn away from you in my misery.*
> *So, I ask you to grant me that special grace to direct the energy of*
>   *my pain,*

as you did in your passion,
to fill the world with love.
Help me to imitate your patience
and to turn my pain into offerings of love for others.
In this time of distress,
I ask, I seek, and I knock,
for the grace of endurance, perseverance,
and above all, trustful acceptance of your divine will.
May thy will be done on Earth in me
for the growth of love among humanity and for your glory.

Carrying a Cross Gracefully

Patient endurance might seem like a tall order, particularly when you are undergoing a great deal of pain. People may tell us that God only sends us the crosses we can bear. Yet a serious illness seems powerful enough to crush us. How often do we willingly embrace our crosses during sickness, especially when there is no end of suffering in sight? It is much easier to admire others who carry their crosses gracefully.

Do you know of people or friends who have endured serious illness or heartbreaking diminishment, yet still remained loving, kind, good-humored, friendly, and helpful? If so, think of them and pray for them, and ask God for the grace to carry your cross patiently and gracefully.

Stage 5

Choice

*When all your strength to resist the diminishment is spent,
you are to unite yourself to the will of God, firmly believing
that the total Body of Christ will ultimately find its
fulfillment through your "offered" diminishments.*

There comes a time, especially in a serious illness or a seemingly permanent life diminishment, when you can no longer resist. Fighting the situation no longer makes much sense. You are forced to acknowledge that you indeed have the illness or disability, whatever it may be, and that it is not likely ever to leave. In this stage of transformation, you may continue praying patiently as in the previous two stages. But here and now, you are faced with major choices.

You must accept the fact that your illness or diminishment is continually weakening you in various ways. Perhaps you can no longer run, or even walk. Perhaps you are quickly fatigued. Perhaps you can no longer digest normal food. Perhaps the pain has grown stronger and more persistent, and never seems to leave. Conditions seem only to get worse. This fact is characteristic of stage 5.

The last of these middle stages of suffering represents a most difficult transitional stage in any lengthy period of diminishment, whether it's a serious illness, a chronic disease, a long-term depression, seemingly endless loneliness, an overpowering addiction, years of abuse, a permanent disability, a frustrating job, or any other diminishment that you realize is never going to go away. Furthermore, you can no longer put up any significant resistance.

Fred in his wheelchair kept thinking that his children and grandchildren wished for him to die, so they could spend all of the money he had so thriftily saved and carefully invested over seventy years. Whenever he tried to pray, he would begin obsessing about what might happen to his money after he died. Images would surface that pictured the various ways his children would squander his hard-earned savings within months after they inherited it. He would debate within himself, wondering if he should change his will. He fantasized about getting even with them by bequeathing all his money to charity.

Teenaged Sarah, suffering from a physical disability that misshaped her spine, came to realize that she would have to live with this disability for the rest of her life. She couldn't help but watch enviously as her classmates went on dates and formed small friendship groups but never invited her. She stood alone near her locker and watched longingly as everyone else seemed to be chatting and laughing together.

It is quite clear that with thoughts like these, it doesn't feel as though your heart's desire is connected to God's heart's desire, and that you have been distracted from your life's purpose during these times.

At moments like these, at every stage of suffering, the challenge is to reconnect to your life's purpose and the most effective use of your suffering energy for the divine purpose. You do this by your choices.

Teilhard sums up the challenge of this stage of suffering. "This is the darkness, heavy with promises and threats, which [you] will have to illuminate and animate with the divine presence."[1] Teilhard is telling you that, although you have been making choices throughout all the stages of your suffering, this is the stage where you make those choices that will transfigure your diminishments into sparkling, shining offerings to God.

Guiding Principles

Teilhard suggests three attitudes for you to adopt at this fifth stage, where making conscious choices becomes of supreme importance.

1. God Transfigures Our Diminishments—Even Our Physical Deaths—by Integrating Them into a Larger, Better Plan, Provided We Lovingly Trust God.

For Teilhard, it is important at this stage that you continue to hold a grand vision of God's project for Earth and creation—a deep longing for the loving union of all creation, which, Jesus assures us, grows quietly, like yeast, in the heart of every human and in every creature. The quiet power of the kingdom of God working in and through all things "is like yeast that a woman took and mixed in with three measures of flour until all of it was leavened" (Luke 13:21).

When you pray the Lord's Prayer and remind yourself that "Thy will be done on Earth," you are affirming that you have committed your life to helping to accomplish God's heart's desire for creation—to being like yeast, quiet yet working powerfully to make a positive difference in fostering God's project. This divine project is far, far bigger than your life, yet your life is meant to contribute toward accomplishing that grand vision of loving union. Teilhard wants you always to keep this bigger plan, God's project, in mind and to remind yourself that you are helping make it happen, even in your suffering.

St. Paul tells us that nothing can withstand the power of God's love and the accomplishment of your special part of God's plan for creation. Christ's love and your love are bound together; they are inseparable.

> Who will separate us from the love of Christ? Will hardship, or distress, or persecution, or famine, or nakedness, or peril, or sword?...No, in all these things we are more than conquerors through him who loved us. For I am convinced that neither death, nor life,...nor anything else in all creation, will be able to separate us from the love of God in Christ Jesus our Lord. (Rom 8:35, 37–39)

2. Suffering Requires
a Tremendous Expenditure of Energy.

If you are at this fifth stage, you probably do not need anyone to tell you that it takes a lot of energy to live with pain day after day, especially knowing that it is not going to go away tomorrow. However, it is important for you to realize the hidden source of power latent in this "tremendous pain energy" that you are generating each day.

As a reminder, Teilhard says that there is no need to undergo unnecessary pain or suffering. Thus, if there is medication you can take to alleviate your pain, he would tell you to take it. Even when physical pain is reduced, there are plenty of other kinds of suffering you can't alleviate with pills—loneliness, frustration, discomfort, limitations, and so on. All this unavoidable emotional and spiritual suffering energy is still available, as fuel, to choose to direct for building the kingdom of God.

3. Consciously "Direct" the Energy.

This is where directing your suffering energy becomes very important—using it wisely and not wasting it. What characterizes stage 5 is that all your strength to resist the diminishment is spent. You can no longer deny that this illness or issue has taken over your life. When this stage is reached, Teilhard suggests, unite yourself to the will of God, firmly believing that God's project will ultimately find its fulfillment through the "directed" choices you make using the energy you generate in your suffering. However, realize that there are many forces at work, very natural and normal ones, that generate more kinds of suffering.

Typically, during this stage, instead of enjoying feelings of peace and connectedness to God and a clear purpose for directing your energy, you may experience feelings of anger, rejection, fear, and helplessness. You may even have thoughts of envy or jealousy toward others who seem not to be diminished as you are, or thoughts of revenge and getting even with those who may have caused your suffering, or thoughts of suicide to escape pain. However, never forget the power of choice.

After a deadly hurricane in Haiti, a young woman physician went there as part of a group of physicians to help. Working in a primitive tent hospital, the doctors faced an endless column of impossible medical problems without proper medicines and instruments. The young doctor felt overwhelmed by the situation. At one point, she said that she became almost paralyzed by her helplessness and fear.

She came to the bedside of a six-year-old boy whose leg had been amputated a few days earlier. Unable to function any longer, she buried her face in her hands and began sobbing. Seeing her teary and trembling, the boy touched her shoulder, smiled at her and encouraged her. He pointed out to her some other kids whom he was sure needed more attention than he did.

In that moment, her overwhelming sense of helplessness was broken open, and she was able to carry on. She had witnessed in that little boy the victory of love over pain and fear. Even deeply suffering people, like this boy, are capable of generosity of heart and compassion. Without realizing it, in his choice for compassion and concern for fellow sufferers, he released her energy, so that both of them in that moment were helping to build the kingdom of God on Earth.

Spiritual Practices for Stage 5

Hopefully, you will continue to use spiritual practices from earlier stages that have brought you insight, awareness, and personal growth. Please continue to use them. Never forget that you have a unique purpose from God to make a positive difference in your world. It is your call from God. No matter how weak or debilitated you may be and no matter how small or insignificant you may feel, God is still calling you to work for the kingdom in whatever ways are still available to you. Paul reminds everyone to think about their life purpose, about their unique calling:

> Consider your own call, brothers and sisters: not many of you were wise by human standards, not many were powerful, not many were of noble birth. But God chose what is foolish in the world to shame the wise; God chose what is weak in the world to shame the strong; God chose what is low and despised in the world, things that are not, to reduce to nothing things that are, so that no one might boast in the presence of God. He is the source of your life in Christ Jesus, who became for us wisdom from God, and righteousness and sanctification and redemption. (1 Cor 1:26–30)

Our Basic Talent

Even though your activities are limited, you still have two ways to fulfill your life purpose. No matter how helpless and forgotten they may be, everyone still has one basic talent given by God to use, the talent of love.

First, you can always show kindness, be grateful, and act courteously. You can always be considerate, accommodating, and forgiving. All these are activities you can still perform within even the most severe diminishment.

Second, because you generate energy in living with your illness or diminishment, you can direct that energy in positive ways.

Very often during these stages of transformation, we are tempted to excuse ourselves from using this basic talent.

Stay Involved

Be committed to your concerns—social, political, and so forth. Write letters to the editor, to your congressperson, and so on. Even if you are sick, you may still be able to use a telephone, a computer, or a tablet. Stay involved with current events. Use what influence you have to make a difference in the world.

Stay involved in the life of your faith community. If you can still attend worship services, do so. Attend any events that seem attractive to you. You can always grow in knowledge and wisdom. If you have enough strength to belong to a church group, keep your membership active, even if you can't participate in its physical activities. In any case, as you read about different liturgical activities, social events, and ministries of mercy in the church bulletin, direct your suffering energy as a prayer for the success of each event.

Make charitable contributions. If you have available money, be generous. Give to needy people or to people who are doing good work, especially in your neighborhood or town. Your charitable contributions offer you the opportunity of continuing your good work, even after you have passed into the fullness of life.

The Bucket List for Making a Difference

Many people make a bucket list of things they would like to do or experience before they die. They list things like "seeing Antarctica," "visiting the Grand Canyon," "winning a million dollars," "publishing a book," "owning a Chevrolet Corvette," and so on. Perhaps, for some, these are the things they want to do.

In contrast, in this bucket list you envision a future where you do things that make a positive difference in your life and in the lives of others. We can't make a list for you, but here are some of the things others have listed as healing items on their bucket lists:

- *Learning to eat mindfully*
- *Volunteering at a soup kitchen*
- *Visiting people randomly at nursing homes*
- *Sending email messages to old friends more frequently*
- *Passing on humorous stories and photos*
- *Being more active on Facebook*
- *Walking at least half a mile three days each week*
- *Affirming family members and friends*
- *Keeping a spiral binder with lists of all the things I'm grateful for*
- *Donating a significant amount of money to charities that I like*
- *Affirming any growth in my consciousness, and talking about these things to my family, especially my children and grand-children*
- *Doing mindfulness meditation each day*
- *Making a list of the things I have learned about life— a "wisdom list"*
- *Reading an inspiring book each month, or more often*
- *Writing a song about loving life*
- *Collecting, organizing, and labeling four boxes of old photographs*
- *Visiting the Holy Land*

The idea is to create your own bucket list with items you know will be healing for you and for those you care about.

Prayer Forms for Stage 5

Hopefully, you are continuing to use prayer forms from earlier stages that have brought you comfort and challenge.

Contemplating the Cross

Reflect prayerfully on each of the statements in these reflections from Cardinal Martini.

The cross is ever before us. It wants to speak to us, if only we contemplate it with love, drawn by the power of the Spirit, who is the gift of Christ crucified. If we look upon it with awe and affection, the cross becomes an enticing, warm and all-consuming fire: it gives us a challenge.

It asks us many things. The cross asks us, our communities, our societies and our cultures to confirm that there do exist paths from the cross to resolve human problems.

Our experience reveals that pain, suffering and death fill our history.

Jesus did not invent the cross. He, like every person, found it on his journey. The newness of his message was to plant a seed of love into our bearing of the cross. The element of love turned the Way of the Cross into a way that leads to life. The cross itself became a message of love; a means of our transformation. Our cross is also the cross of Jesus![2]

Living Your Wounds

Reflect prayerfully on each of the statements in these thoughts from Henri Nouwen:

The great challenge is living your wounds through, instead of thinking them through. It is better to cry than to worry, better to feel your wounds deeply than to understand them, better to let them into your silence than to talk about them.

The choice you face constantly is whether you are taking your wounds to your head or to your heart. In your head you can analyze them….But no final healing is likely to come from that source. You need to let your wounds go down to your heart. Then you can live through them and discover that they will not destroy you. Your heart is greater than your wounds.[3]

Prayer of Those Who Are Incomplete

In your prayer, find ways to acknowledge that as a created being you are still incomplete, and that every other incomplete being around you is striving for its own completeness. Earth itself and everything on it is still incomplete, still in a state of process. Furthermore, this universal incompleteness that is striving to become complete produces unavoidable suffering for everyone involved.

A Meditative Prayer for Stage 5

God transfigures our diminishments—even our physical deaths—by integrating them into a larger, better plan, provided we lovingly trust God.

I am not having a good time, Holy One.
This pain is sucking all my energy.
I am tempted to be angry, and rage against the
stabs of pain.
May I convert the energy of my rage
into something that brings me closer to You.
May I realize that all this is You, in some way,
that all this takes place in You,
that all this is happening within a much grander
scheme of things,
which I don't attempt to understand.

Part Three

STAGES
OF UNION

As mentioned earlier, Teilhard's seven stages of suffering are not to be confused with the typical stages of death and dying—denial, anger, bargaining, depression, and acceptance—as found in Elizabeth Kubler-Ross's classic text *On Death and Dying*. You do not have to be dying—or even sick—to enter these two highest stages of suffering, since there are many kinds of suffering that do not involve being ill or diseased. There are millions of people worldwide suffering religious or political persecution; millions of grieving people; hundreds of thousands who are unemployed and in anguish because they cannot support their families; countless suffer failure, rejection, ostracism, loneliness, hunger, and abuse each day. No one group has an exclusive claim on suffering.

Rather than stages of dying, Teilhard's seven stages reflect stages of spiritual growth that may occur among any suffering individuals who are in love with both God and our evolving world.

This double love—of God *and* the world—that Teilhard promotes is in contrast to traditional spirituality, which demands an either/or commitment: you either love God or you love the world, but you can't love both; if you love one, you must hate the other. Teilhard insists that, as a basic tenet of spirituality today, we are called to love *passionately* both God *and* the world God created.

Thus, for Teilhard, there are two equally primary functions of an evolutionary spirituality: first, a personal spiritual development and love of God, and second, the spiritual development of collective humanity and love of God's creation.

During the first half of the twentieth century when Teilhard lived, it was hard to find many Christians who believed that humans were involved in a grand evolutionary project initiated and guided by God. Rather, most viewed life on Earth as little more than a testing period to see if they could avoid sin, patiently endure suffering, escape hell, and make it into heaven.

Today, perhaps with fuller understanding of our evolving universe, it may be possible for many more to discover they could aspire to both these final two higher stages of evolutionary spirituality.

Other than Teilhard himself, it is hard to find examples of such evolved consciousness. However, in their own day, two examples that seem to anticipate this level of spiritual growth might be St. Francis of Assisi and St. Thérèse of Lisieux: St. Francis, with his passionate love of and personal relation to creation as an expression of God's life, anticipating Teilhard's Divine Milieu; and St. Thérèse, with her realization that she could direct the energy of both her work and her suffering, through her prayerful intention, to support the efforts of missionaries working in foreign lands. For Thérèse's innovations in spirituality and spiritual practices, which she called "The Little Way," she was named a "doctor" (teacher) of the church and also patron of foreign missionaries, even though in her entire religious life she never left the confines of her Carmelite convent in France.

We have renamed these last two stages of suffering *stages of union*, even though a key word used in Teilhard's descriptions of stages 6 and 7 is *resignation*. He describes stage 6 as "communion with God in resignation." In using the term *resignation*, Teilhard is focused on people's relation to their illness, disease, or other diminishments that cause their suffering. Teilhard's point is that, at this stage, the sufferer is "resigned" to the fact that this illness or diminishment is not going to go away, that it may remain a lifelong presence, and that they may find a purpose for their life in and through suffering.

In labeling these final stages of suffering as stages of union, we have chosen to more accurately focus them on the individual's spiritual growth, since not all sufferers attain these two final stages. Some never quite make it through the stages of transformation; some remain fixed at the resistance stages, fighting their illness till their last breath.

For those at these highest stages of spiritual growth, paradoxically, even though their pain and suffering may be at its most intense, it is no longer of major concern. These people have reached a deep union with God (stage 6) and manifest a total commitment to the fullest development of the cosmic Body of Christ (stage 7).

It is difficult to separate stage 6 from stage 7 as they represent two sides, or functions, of an evolutionary spirituality: *personal spiritual growth* and *love of God* (stage 6) and commitment to the *collective spiritual growth* of humanity and *love of creation* (stage 7).

Stage 6 emphasizes your communion with God, a communion that exists and flourishes over and above your ongoing suffering and diminishment. In this stage, you are no longer focused on your pain, discomfort, inabilities, or frustrations, but on aligning your heart with God's heart. You might express it as "I live in God and God lives in me." Of course, we can all speak that sentence as an intellectual assent or an act of faith, but the person at stage 6 knows, sees, and feels the reality of it.

Stage 7 emphasizes the sufferer's fidelity or faithfulness to the work of the growth of the Body of Christ even while bearing his or her diminishments. For the person in stage 7, one's suffering is no longer seen as a burden and one is no longer struggling against it, since everything is now focused on pushing open the envelope of evolutionary growth of the human family in the Divine Milieu. All one's remaining energy and attention is directed to fulfilling God's heart's desire for Earth and the fullest development of the Body of Christ. The person at stage 7 might say, "God's heart's desire for Earth has become my heart's desire."

Once the struggle against illness and diminishments is no longer the focus of attention, sufferers at stage 7 see their primary purpose for being alive as helping to build the Body of Christ, or God's project. They do it primarily by redirecting the energy expended in their suffering to renewing the face of the Earth.

Perhaps, now, with this clarification, we can begin to explore the guiding principles, spiritual practices, and prayer forms appropriate to these two stages of union.

Stage 6

Communion

*When you are resigned to the fact that your diminishment
may remain a lifelong presence, join God in communion
across (over and above) the diminishment at a level
of union stronger than the diminishment.*

To reach these final two stages of suffering, it is important to emphasize that you do not have to be near death. They do not describe the
final stages of dying, but rather higher stages of spiritual life and
development in evolutionary consciousness.

St. Paul described stage 6 when he wrote of the Divine Milieu
as a glorification of Christ, and assured his followers that it may
indeed become theirs "if, in fact, we suffer with him so that we may
also be glorified with him" (Rom 8:17).

Paradoxically, for those at these highest stages of spiritual
growth, even though their pain and suffering may be at its most
intense, it is no longer of major concern. Such people have reached
a deep union with God, where their pain and suffering take second
place in their concern. They are willing to let God shape them in any
way God may wish. Teilhard describes it this way:

> Like an artist who is able to make use of a fault or an
> impurity in the stone he is sculpting or the bronze he is
> casting so as to produce more exquisite lines or a more
> beautiful tone, God, without sparing us the partial deaths,
> nor the final death, which form an essential part of our
> lives, transfigures them by integrating them in a better
> plan—provided we lovingly trust in him.[1]

Guiding Principles

1. Stay in Union with God, with Christ, and with Those Working toward the Betterment of the World.

There are many ways to practice Teilhard's first principle for stage 6 and "stay in union with God." Most likely, you already have developed your personal ways of staying in the loving presence of God.

It is evident that many may not have been raised with an image of the Creator or heavenly God as infinitely loving and all-embracing, and thus prefer, at this stage, to focus on their union with Christ, since they have many loving images of him. Some prefer to picture the Sacred Heart of Jesus with their heart joined to his heart. Others prefer to picture him as an adult on Earth preaching and healing, or even as a baby in the manger (one of St. Augustine's favorite images). Still others, in receiving holy communion, picture themselves in union with others in the Body of Christ working for the betterment of the world. A few may even have a kind of cosmic image of Christ. Use whatever image helps your experience of union.

The main point is to begin to love God—using whatever images you prefer—and to let that love become passionate and all-absorbing. Let it become so absorbing that relieving your pain and suffering, which used to be the focus of your concern, takes a much lower place of importance in your life. God is at the center of your stage now. However, even at this intensity of union with God, Teilhard does not want you to waste the energy your body and mind generate in pain and suffering.

2. Continue to Let Your Diminishments Be Transfigured into a Force That Helps Build the Body Of Christ.

Hopefully, during the early stages of your suffering, you *learned many ways to let your diminishment energy be redirected into a force that helps build the Body of Christ.* So, here too, Teilhard reminds you that, even in your deepest experience of union with God or Christ, you still have a purpose and a commitment to use your suffering energy for the healing of our planet and the spiritual growth of the human race.

Since the transformation of Earth is seen primarily as the work of the Holy Spirit, alignment—or union—with this divine Spirit might be another way of staying in union with God.

Despite your almost total absorption with God and God's love, it is important at this stage that you continue to practice generosity, show gratitude for everything and toward everyone, maintain a sense of humor, give affirmations freely, forgive freely, and spread joy.

Spiritual Practices for Stage 6

Nurturing Joy and Humor

Joy is a spiritual energy. Like faith, it has a kind of unshakeable permanence. Joy is to be distinguished from happiness, which is an emotional energy that comes and goes depending on feelings of the moment. You can be interiorly joyful and at peace, even in times of unhappiness or adversity. Joy comes from knowing that you, personally, are unconditionally loved and embraced by God. Joy is a spiritual state that no amount of pain can take from you. Even as Jesus was predicting that his disciples would have to suffer, his prayer was "that my joy may be in you, and that your joy may be complete" (John 15:11).

Alex was a great example of maintaining a sense of humor. He was under home hospice care during his last few months, dying of complications from melanoma. Each Thursday, a hospice volunteer would telephone him to see if he needed any medical supplies or prescription drugs over the weekend. When the hospice volunteer phoned to ask if he needed anything, he would typically reply with humor: "A bottle of vodka" or "A case of beer" or "A pretty young woman" or "A new liver." He would then laugh and tell the volunteer how nice she was to call him.

A Butterfly Ride

Your imagination is the most all-encompassing faculty you possess. It has the ability to integrate within it your body, mind, and spirit and can locate you anywhere in the universe, in the past, present, or the future.

This information about the imaginative faculty should not come as a surprise, since you probably have been using your imagination in this integrative way since childhood. How many children, while lying in their bed on a cold winter's night, have imagined playing in warm sand by the lake the way they did last summer? How many young brides to be, many months before their wedding, envisioned walking down the aisle at church? How many young couples holding hands have imagined sitting in a new home or rocking a future child in their arms? This service of carrying us to desired scenes is provided very simply and naturally by that special faculty called your imagination.

In an earlier stage in the suffering process, you learned to use your imagination to relieve your pain by having it take you back to a happy scene, and to bring it to life again using all the "senses" of your imagination—sight, hearing, touch, taste, and smell, as well as your positive emotional state at the time—in order to distract you from the pain being experienced by your body. In these activities, you learned to "leave your body" and to go to a more pleasurable time and place.

In this exercise, rather than retreat in time or advance to the future, you will learn to experience the present in a new way. Using your imagination, you can either fly somewhere as a butterfly or you can ride on the back of a great butterfly in its flight.

This process is designed to teach you how to leave your body. With a little practice, you can learn to leave your body at will and for as long as you wish.

The best time to practice this "butterfly ride" is when you are not in serious pain, so that you will know how to leave your body easily when you are in serious pain. During stages 6 and 7, people are often in deep physical pain, a level where even strong pain medications can't seem to achieve their desired effect. That is where this activity becomes very useful.

Here are the steps:

Butterfly Ride

1. Close your eyes and let yourself grow quietly centered. (If you have developed a process you prefer for growing quiet,

use it again and again; that is the way to condition yourself so that you are able to get centered as quickly and as easily as possible.)

2. Begin to use your imagination to picture yourself on the ceiling of the room you are in, looking down on your body in a bed or chair. Though your body in the bed or chair may be in pain, notice that the you on the ceiling is free of pain.

3. Look around until you see (in imagination) a butterfly somewhere in the room. Carefully describe in detail the butterfly and where in the room it is waiting for you.

4. Situate yourself near the butterfly. You may wish to imagine yourself becoming a butterfly and accompanying the butterfly in its journey, or you may choose to ride on the butterfly's back and soar through the sky wherever it takes you.

5. Take off. As you are flying together across the sky, notice the scenes beneath you. Comment on them and describe them to your butterfly companion.

6. Continue journeying all over the city or the world— or beyond Earth. When you are ready to return to your suffering body, you may do so.

As a relative, friend, or caregiver, you may sometimes encounter dying people who wish to die but cannot seem to do it. They can't seem to let go of physical life. They can't seem to leave their bodies. You may teach them this process of leaving one's body. For such people, this enjoyable butterfly ride shows them a simple way to leave their bodies and let go of their physical life.

Prayer Forms for Stage 6

Many of the practices and prayer forms that you learned in earlier stages are still appropriate in this stage, though their content and focus might need adjusting. For example, the words of your mantra prayers may change and become simpler as your awareness of God's presence deepens and intensifies. Mantra prayers are always easy ones to use, especially if your physical energies are limited or your days are full of distractions. Furthermore, do not forget to renew your fundamental choice to live as healthily as you can today.

Thanksgiving Examen

The human heart in union with God lives in a state of continual gratitude. While traditional spirituality encourages people to do an examination of conscience at bedtime to see how one may have offended God, Teilhard would encourage sufferers rather to spend this time in expressing gratitude for the blessings of the day.

People who are very ill or under severe diminishment will come to notice the smallest things to be grateful for—the ability to breathe, to drink or sip water, to give or receive a smile, to dress oneself, to use the bathroom, to laugh, to sit up, to use one's voice, and so on. These are things healthy people simply take for granted, but for those in the throes of suffering, these are precious abilities.

Suzanne had only a short time to live, as she was suffering from a rare mitochondrial disease that, little by little, drained energy from each cell in her body. On the Internet, she started a Care Page for people who had similar diseases, and others who wished to visit the Web site. She encouraged her Care Page companions to develop an attitude of gratitude. She modeled the Thanksgiving Examen for them. On her daily entry she might write, "Today I was able to put my feet into the community swimming pool," or, "Today I was able to eat and digest a small meatball," or, "Today a puppy sat on my lap and licked my fingers," or, "Today my husband wheeled me out to the bay to watch the sunset, and I was able to take some photos of it," or, "Today the hospice worker came and we sang songs together," or, "Today my husband hooked my computer up to the large television screen, so even with my poor eyesight I could read what people wrote on my Care Page."

Thanking Your Body

The organs and systems of your physical body are doing the best they can at this point. If you can imagine your heart or kidney or liver talking to you, ask them how they are doing and thank them for their continual service to you. They are the ones who know you intimately; they suffer and rejoice with you. Tell them how you yearn to be in union with God while still lovingly in your body.

Instant and Continuous Communion

This prayer is for those who may not be able to participate in eucharistic celebrations.

By faith, we know that everything, even the air we breathe, exists and moves and has its being in God. Teilhard called this field of life and energy we live in the Divine Milieu. It permeates everything, gives life to every cell in our bodies, and gives its life and love to all the particles floating in the air. So every time we inhale, we are inhaling particles, mostly so small they are invisible. Yet every particle participates in Christ's life and God's life. The Holy Spirit is sanctifying every one of those particles at every moment. If, at this stage of union with God, you can let yourself realize this, you can take holy communion with every breath.

One way to do this with full consciousness is, first, to use your imagination to picture Christ in front of you in the air in the room; second, as you inhale, to welcome Christ into yourself; and third, to repeat this inhalation of Christ with each subsequent breath.

To do this spiritual practice, use whatever imagery feels most natural to you. You may picture Christ entering you through your nose or mouth or just permeating through your skin or going directly to your heart. Find some way that feels spontaneously right. For example, in this special communion, you may prefer simply to imagine Christ giving you a holy kiss, to show his love for you and his reverent respect for your physical body.

Jesus' Last Words

Reflect on Jesus' last words on the cross and find ways to apply them to your situation.

- *"Father, forgive them; for they do not know what they are doing" (Luke 23:34).*

  Talk to God or Christ about some acts of forgiveness that you have done in the past and how it felt to forgive—or about some forgiveness you still have yet to give or receive.

- *"Truly I tell you, today you will be with me in Paradise"* *(Luke 23:43).*

    Affirm your faith in God. Affirm that you know you are safely in God's loving hands at this moment and at every moment.

- *"Woman, here is your son"* *(John 19:26).*

    Regarding your illness or diminishment, are there some matters that need to be taken care of? Do you need to complete your will? Are you responsible for the care of someone? Talk to God about these issues.

- *"Here is your mother"* *(John 19:27).*

    Do you need to assign responsibility to someone for something you had been planning to do? Is there some project in your life that still needs completion?

- *"My God, my God, why have you forsaken me?"* *(Matthew 27:46; Mark 15:34)*

    This is the opening line of Psalm 22. If Jesus quietly recites the rest of the psalm to himself on the cross, the psalm ends with a deep trust in God. It's okay to feel that God has abandoned you; Jesus probably felt it too. Forgive yourself, and ask for the grace to restore your faith in the loving care of God. Prayerfully read the entire psalm.

- *"I am thirsty"* *(John 19:28).*

    It is okay to have physical thirst. It is okay to express your felt needs. You may also have some emotional or spiritual thirst. Can you identify what you yearn for or long for? Do you have some deep unfulfilled desire? Can you express it to God?

- *"It is finished"* *(John 19:30).*

    Talk to God about the fact that you are finished fighting this illness or diminishment, that you are resigned to accept it as a part of your life for the rest of your life, and that you will find ways to use each day and each moment in ways that would please God.

• *"Father, into your hands I commend my spirit" (Luke 23:46).*
These last words from Luke can be your mantra
prayer during days of sickness and diminishment.

A Meditative Prayer for Stage 6

There is nothing more I can do.
There is nothing more the doctors can do.
There is nothing more that comfort and love
can accomplish.
The end is nearing, I know.
At times I can barely stay conscious.
I turn myself entirely over to You
in trust.
I wish to be in intimate communion with You,
in the Cosmic Christ.
I have no idea how any of this unfolds,
but I believe that my pain is transformative
for me and for others.
Transform me now, O Cosmic Love
into what I am to become.

Stage 7

Fidelity

Let your deepest communion with God coincide with your deepest fidelity to the human task of promoting complexity and consciousness and the completion of God's project.

❁

Although there are many mystics throughout history that reflect Teilhard's stage 6 in their intense loving union with the Divine, it is difficult to find many that truly "qualify" for his stage 7, which calls for a passionate love of creation. Perhaps it is because few, if any, of the mystics before Teilhard could have been aware of creation in its evolutionary process and concerned about a positive future for Earth that needs to be loved into existence. The mysticism of stage 7 is relatively new and merits some description here.

In Teilhard's spirituality, two of his central evolutionary principles were first to love the "invisible" and second to love the "not yet."

Loving the Invisible

For most of us, it is easy to love what is visible in creation—our family, friends, pets, flowers, trees, lakes, and even the clouds, the moon, and the stars. However, what about loving the invisible atoms of oxygen in the air, the photosynthesis process happening in the leaves, the thousands of species of bacteria that live in your stomach and help digest the food you eat so that it nourishes you, or the billions of cells throughout your body that make up your immune system? Did you know that there are about three thousand sensory nerve endings on each of your fingertips? All these are mostly invisible to the naked eye. For Teilhard, these invisible workings are meant to be the recipients of our love and gratitude.

Furthermore, among other invisible things that he recommends for our love and gratitude are thoughts, ideas, insights, desires, dreams, plans, hopes, worries, or fears—in our own minds or the minds of others. Can you recall watching and loving the dawning awareness and mental capacities in a child—the ability to read and comprehend sentences in a book, to print and write one's name, and to memorize the multiplication table? Teilhard loves the realization that happens when someone discovers that they can create, that they can envision a future and make it happen—such as a personal accomplishment, a goal to be achieved, a project to be completed.

Loving the Not Yet

Loving the invisible leads to loving the not yet—those things that have yet to be discovered and invented, so that humans may become more aware, more conscious, more loving, and more all-embracing. We would still be traveling by horse and stagecoach if someone late in the nineteenth century had not envisioned the not yet automobile. The same goes for those who envisioned the airplane, the radio, the telephone, the television, and the computer when they were still a not yet.

In the healing arts, someone had to envision and create the not yet (which is "now" for us) such as vitamin pills, inoculations, antiseptics, antibiotics, pain-reducing drugs, laser surgery, X-ray, CT scans, MRIs, and a whole host of other drugs and technological tools that enhance our health.

Some people in a tribal community thousands of years ago had to envision a not yet democratic way of governing. People in nations had to envision a not yet single worldwide governing body like the United Nations.

There was a time when schools, libraries, hospitals, Medicare, social security, and supermarkets were all not yets. People had to envision them and want them enough to make them real.

Who better than those who suffer and love God to envision something that is not yet and begin to love it into existence with their suffering energy? Who better than a person with cancer to envision a world in the not yet where cancer can be cured? Who better than persons with debilitating diseases like Parkinson to envision a not yet where cures for their diseases have been found? Who better than those suffering from self-destructive addictions to envision a not yet where successful treatments can be found? Who better than those suffering from chronic unemployment to envision a not yet where those who want to work can find jobs that provide purpose and fulfillment for their talents and skills?

Teilhard says that you can direct all the energy generated in your suffering toward goals like these. Those goals may not be achieved in your lifetime, but in your love for the people not yet born, you are willing to invest your active energy as well as your passive suffering to benefit the world that is not yet.

At stage 7 of suffering, your prayers are now focused on "Thy will be done on Earth." This is evolutionary prayer. That statement in the Lord's Prayer is about the not yet. In the original Aramaic version of that prayer, which is the language in which Jesus first announced it, that statement conveys this sense: "May your heart's desire, God, become our hearts' desire." May we desire for the not yet exactly what you, God, desire for it.

The expression "Thy kingdom come!" is also a desire for the not yet, especially since God's rule of love for Earth has not yet penetrated all the hearts of the human family in a way that would have created one loving planet-wide family.

Loving the invisible and the not yet is what Teilhard envisions for the people at stage 7—that you, within your suffering and your union with God, would redirect your suffering energies toward the evolutionary consciousness God wants and desires for us and from us.

Stage 7 moves beyond stage 6, for in the earlier stage you might tend to rest in your loving union with God—alone and beyond your suffering; dealing with your pain is no longer of major importance, since all your attention is on union with God.

In stage 7, you realize that God's larger focus is on the not yet of creation—the evolution, which still needs to happen in human hearts on Earth, of bringing the fullness of life to humanity. While remaining in God's presence (stage 6), you choose to refocus all your love and suffering energy toward "renewing the face of the Earth."

You realize that God loves the world so much because God's beloved Son has incorporated the whole world into his cosmic body. God wants everyone and everything that is part of the Son's cosmic body to become fully conscious of who they are and what they have become in this divine incorporation. Furthermore, although that full realization is at present far from being achieved, you want to focus all of your strength, love, and energy toward the fulfillment of God's yet-unfulfilled desire for creation.[1]

The description of stage 7 is paradoxical. If you are fulfilling your greatest desire and enjoying a deep communion with God, how can there be anything more? The answer is that God has a much bigger desire for you. In your blissful union with the divinity, God asks that God's heart's desire become the focus of your loving attention. Love what God loves. Love God more fully by loving the object of God's heart's desire. Instead of just loving God with all your heart and soul and "hating" the world, Teilhard invites you to discover that you can love both God and the world passionately. He makes this shift very specific in his principles and practices for this stage of suffering.

Guiding Principles

1. The Primary Purpose for Being Alive Is to Help Build the Body of Christ—The Kingdom of God.

There are at least two reasons Teilhard can say you are called to love the world passionately. The first is because God the Creator loved creation as much as God loved his own Son, Jesus the Christ (see John 3:16–17). The second is because Christ in his resurrected body assumed all creation into his body and became the Cosmic or Universal Christ. And that cosmic body, which is the Divine Milieu, has yet to enter into fullest consciousness of what it truly is, and the creatures in that cosmic milieu have yet to learn to live with one another in peace and all-embracing love. Helping achieve that state of consciousness and love is what is meant when we say "to help build the Body of Christ," also referred to by Jesus as the kingdom of God or the kingdom of heaven. "Thy kingdom come."

2. Direct the Energy You Expend in Suffering to Promote Growth in Love of the Planet.

Previously, people believed they could help build the Body of Christ (God's project) only by the physical effort of their work, performing the works of justice and mercy, advancing medicine and technology, making the world a better place by their creativity and labor. Teilhard says we can also be making the world a better place with our suffering, by directing the energy generated in suffering to accomplish the same purpose as our physical effort and work.

Recalling his experiences during wartime as a stretcher bearer, Teilhard knew that there are always soldiers who are wounded or killed during a victorious battle, and he applies that experience to those who suffer and die in serving God's plan for the eventual fulfillment of the divine desire. "God does not therefore suffer a preliminary defeat in our defeat because," Teilhard explains, "although we appear to succumb individually," God's project will ultimately triumph "through our deaths" and we will live again to enjoy that triumph.[2]

In St. Paul's words, "I appeal to you therefore, brothers and sisters, by the mercies of God, to present your bodies as a living sacrifice, holy and acceptable to God, which is your spiritual worship" (Rom 12:1).

3. Direct All Your Energy to Drive Evil Away so That Nothing in Creation Is Diminished.

True resignation at this stage means letting go of all expectation of a cure or relief from your suffering, and rather focusing on what God wants you to accomplish—"Thy will be done on Earth." Enjoyment of your union with God (stage 6) requires no expenditure of energy on your part, since that union is purely a gift of the Divine Spirit. So, what are you to do with all your suffering energy? In stage 7, your very love for God and God's desire for Earth leads you to direct all that energy to help produce the fullness of life, consciousness, and love on Earth and to remove all diminishments. You do this in union with all the other creative forces in the world as well as with "the creative force" (the Holy Spirit).

103

Spiritual Practices for Stage 7

Live out your primary purpose in life through suffering as well as through your physical and mental efforts in performing works of justice, mercy, and creativity by directing the energy you expend in suffering to promote Earth's development.

Here Teilhard reminds you that there are always two sources of energy that you have at your disposal: first, the energy of your activities of daily life by which you directly affect the world in a positive way, and second, the energy you expend in suffering. Teilhard says you can redirect your suffering energy in general or for a specific person or project.

Direct all your energy in a general way, as "in union with the creative force of the world," or direct it to a specific creative force, as to this team of people helping to build a house or to a team of researchers searching for a cure for cancer. If you have a specific creative project toward which you would like to direct your energy, you may do that too.

Teilhard points out that it is better for us to consciously choose the objects and creative forces on the planet that will receive the energy of our suffering, instead of just vaguely disseminating it. The more we are involved in the object and objective of our choices, the more intensely focused will be our use of energy.

Union with All Things

By faith, we know that everything exists and moves in the Divine Milieu, as do all the particles in the air we breathe. From science, we know that the particles in the air, following the wind currents, eventually circle the entire globe. Thus, particles that people in East Asia exhaled two weeks ago will be part of the atmosphere in North America today. These are particles that lived and experienced life in another human being, animal, or plant a few weeks ago, and they carry with them some effect of the sadness or joy felt by those creatures at that time.

The air you breathe also carries with it the particles exhaled by the people, the pets, the birds, the trees around you—even the dust of the road, the automobile exhaust, the scent of the flowers, as well as all the various chemicals in the atmosphere.

The fact is that elements of God's project fill the air that you breathe. Each time you inhale, you are taking into you millions of tiny, invisible particles that have come from somewhere outside of you—your room, your home, your family members, your visitors, your neighborhood, your town, your nation, and the entire world.

Furthermore, those same particles are the very particles that have been recycled a million times throughout Earth's history. Some of them were once in Jesus of Nazareth, in famous and ordinary men and women in past years and centuries.

With every breath, then, you take in many particles that have helped build the Christ project over the years. With every breath, you identify yourself with the Christ project. You inhale it into your own body and give it life. In this kind of holy communion, you are in union with the Christ project. You love it. You energize it. You bestow upon it the energy of your suffering.

To practice this communion with the God project, first use your imagination to picture some phase or activity of the God project that is dear to you; visualize it happening there in front of you. Perhaps it is someone undergoing surgery. Perhaps it is a student struggling with an examination. Perhaps it is a group of hungry children somewhere in the world. Perhaps it is someone in a laboratory searching for a new vaccine. This activity can be happening anywhere in the world, for among those particles you are about to inhale, some of them have come from the persons or work you want to bless. Then, as you inhale, take that scene into your body with love. Embrace it. Fill it with warmth and strength. Give it energy. Bless it. Do lovingly whatever feels right.

If you have invested your caring in a dozen different parts of the God project, you can send the energy of your suffering into each of them. You can repeat this communion with the God project for each of your cares, each time using images that evoke that event.

Prayer Forms for Stage 7

Prayer of Gratitude

Although at this stage you may be physically diminished, hopefully, God's heart's desire for Earth has also become your heart's desire, and you are directing and aiming all the energy you produce through your suffering that God's desires for creation may be fulfilled.

One of the more powerful and selfless prayers you can perform at this stage is the prayer of gratitude. It is a powerful way to release all your remaining attachments, and focus on God's unending love for you.

Mother Teresa often told this story about her earliest day working among the poor and dying on the streets of Calcutta:

One evening, she and a small group of sisters were walking along the street and picked up four people to take back to their house and care for them. Finding the one who was in the worst shape, she told the sisters to take care of the others and she would tend to this woman.

Mother Teresa reported, "I did for her all that my love could do. As I put her in bed, there was such a beautiful smile on her face. She took hold of my hand and said only: *Thank you.* And she died."

As she stood there, the good sister began to examine her own thoughts. She asked herself, "What would I have said if I had been in her place?" Reflecting honestly, she realized she would have tried to draw a little attention to herself, saying things like, "I am hungry. I am dying. I am in pain," or something like that. But this dying woman gave her much more. She gave Mother Teresa grateful love. And she died with a smile on her face.[3]

The realization here is that, before God, we are all basically recipients. Everything is gift. God does not owe us anything. We deserve nothing, yet we have all that we have as gift. As one wise man has observed, "The opposite of humility is not pride, but ingratitude." Humility is to realize how blessed we have been, despite the diminishments we have had to endure during life. No one understands the true meaning of humility better than persons in the last stages of life, like this woman that Mother Teresa found on the streets of Calcutta. Persons at this stage cannot even take their next breath for granted.[4]

The Little Way

One of the easiest and best ways to transform your ordinary actions is to follow what St. Thérèse of Lisieux called her "Little Way." It is a "way" of living where *you do each little thing—no matter how boring or distasteful—with love and care.* It is a "way" we can all adopt and make a small contribution to renewing the face of our Earth.

To all sufferers who feel that they can do nothing big or impressive, St. Thérèse is a reminder that it is the little things done with loving care that keep God's project moving forward and hold God's world together. Without millions of small acts of love and caring that people do every day, it is likely the human race would quickly fall apart. Thérèse understood that what matters in life is not great deeds, but great love, and that anyone can achieve the heights of spirituality and help transform the world by doing even the smallest things well for love of God.

Her daily life in the convent was made up of many little things, most of them tedious and boring: weeding the garden, peeling potatoes in the kitchen, dusting the convent stairs, sewing and mending torn clothing, cleaning the animal stalls, scrubbing sinks, sweeping the corridors, gathering and preparing vegetables, cleaning the bedpans of the sick nuns, listening to the older nuns tell the same stories over and over, and so on. It is in this context of doing a thousand little things that Thérèse discovered and practiced her Little Way.

Her Little Way is quite simple, but not always easy. Anyone can follow it. It applies primarily to activities that may be routine and dreary. It applies to tedious conversations and interactions, wherever you may be. It applies to every conversation, no matter how unimportant. It applies to every facet and moment of your life.

Here are the steps of her "Little Way":

- *Do each step or element of your daily life with the intention of pleasing God and helping further God's plan just a little bit more.*
- *Do each little action as an expression of your love for God, for humanity, and for God's Earth.*
- *If you do it with love in your heart—no matter what it is—*

you can be confident that it is helping carry out what God wants of you. It is a part of God's plan and God's plan for you.

- *If you fail or miss a chance to do something in a loving way, know that God still loves you infinitely and forgives you before you even realize it.*
- *If you err, just smile, say thanks to God for God's love and forgiveness, and go back to your daily duties as lovingly as you can.*

Following this Little Way of loving creates a ceaseless flow of love—back and forth—between Creator and creature. Once you let yourself feel this interchange of love, it does away with the feeling that to please God you must do great and extraordinary things.

A Meditative Prayer for Stage 7

As far as I can tell, it is over:
I do not belong to myself any longer (if I ever did!).
I belong entirely to You.
You have taken over my transition.
As You summon me from this human existence,
may I leave behind what needs to be left behind,
so that I am unencumbered to return to You.
I sever my ties
with all that has brought me joy in this world,
and yet I carry them with me in You.
I forgive all those who have hurt me.
I ask forgiveness
for everything I have ever done that has brought pain.
I bless all the loved ones I leave behind.
May I bring to You what You had hoped I might.
May my compassion be deep enough
that I might serve Your compassionate purposes
in the next stage of my existence.
May I continue to serve
in union with all the other creative forces of the Universe.
May it be so.

A Final Comment

Although people often describe life with God in heaven as a time of "eternal rest," it seems quite obvious that everyone there, including angels, saints, and our loved ones, are kept busy interceding for the needs of those on Earth. Most likely, when we pass on to that heavenly state, we too will want to be busy as ever. We will still be saying, "Thy will be done on Earth," and we will be using every bit of heavenly energy and influence we have to inspire people on Earth to keep making a positive difference with their lives, so that God's plan may eventually reach its loving, all-embracing fullness of completion that the Creator intended from the start.

Notes

Introduction

1. Taken from Pierre Teilhard de Chardin, *The Hymn of the Universe* (New York: Perennial Library, Harper & Row, 1961), 94.

2. You will not find a list of these seven stages of suffering anywhere in Teilhard's writings. We have carefully distilled our source material for the seven stages from a number of his essays, but mostly from an extended section describing a positive human response to evil and diminishments, developed in his spirituality book *The Divine Milieu*, especially in part 2: "The Divinization of Our Passivities." It is clear from pages in *The Divine Milieu* that Teilhard regards those who suffer as invited to grow through progressive stages of spiritual growth in line with his evolutionary principles. Though he does not number these stages, he clearly describes them as stages or steps in a process of growth available to a sufferer. See also Pierre Teilhard de Chardin, "The Meaning and Constructive Value of Suffering," in *Teilhard de Chardin: Pilgrim of the Future*, ed. Neville Braybrooke, trans. Noel Lindsay (New York: Seabury Press, 1964), 23–26; and "Mass on the World," composed in 1923, in *Hymn of the Universe*.

3. As a closing prayer for each of the seven stages, we present reflective thoughts written especially for these stages and this book by Teilhardian Andre Auger, of Guelph, Ontario, in Canada.

Essential Perspectives

1. A fuller development of Teilhard's Law of Attraction-Connection-Complexity-Consciousness may be found in Louis M. Savary, *Teilhard de Chardin—The Divine Milieu Explained: A Spirituality for*

the 21st Century (New York: Paulist Press, 2007), 29–30, and *The New Spiritual Exercises* (New York: Paulist Press, 2010), 17ff. See also his essay "Expanding Teilhard's 'Complexity-Consciousness' Law," in *Teilhard Studies* 68 (Spring 2014), http://teilharddechardin.org/mm_uploads/68-Expanding_Teilhards_Complexity-Consciousness_Law.pdf.

2. Teilhard discovered the theological foundation for his positive and evolutionary understanding of human suffering in St. Paul's writings. In many places, Paul explains how his (Paul's) personal sufferings benefit *others as well as himself* (Eph 3:13; Col 1:24; Phil 1:19–21; 3:8–11; 2 Cor 12:7–10); *the believing community* (2 Tim 2:10–12; Rom 8:17–18, 28), and *the Body of Christ* (2 Tim 2:3, 9; 1 Cor 1:18; 2 Cor 4:8–10; Gal 2:20; 6:14, 17). More recently, Pope John Paul II's apostolic letter *Salvivici doloris* (The Life-Giving Power of Suffering), shows how St. Paul clearly affirms that when we humans suffer, we participate in and help complete Christ's work of redemption and salvation. The pope adds, "Christ has also *raised human suffering to the level of the Redemption.* Thus each person, in his or her suffering, can also become a sharer in the redemptive suffering of Christ" (19).

The Significance of Suffering

1. From a 1947 essay "Reflections on Original Sin" in Pierre Teilhard de Chardin, *Christianity and Evolution* (New York: Mariner Books, 2002), 187.

2. Teilhard would exempt from this rule situations where one's purpose is skill training or healing treatment, as in the painful discipline required in the mastery of any art form or sporting ability, or in healing, as the expected painful side effects of certain required medical treatments.

3. Teilhard de Chardin, "Reflections on Original Sin," 66.

4. Ibid., 72.

PART ONE: Stages of Resistance

1. Pierre Teilhard de Chardin, *The Divine Milieu* (New York: Harper Collins, 1965), 84.

Stage 1. Outer Resistance

1. Teilhard de Chardin, *The Divine Milieu*, 83–84.

2. *Ibid.*, 83.

3. *Ibid.*, 84.

4. Dr. Bernie Siegel, MD, wrote a famous book about illness, called *Love, Medicine and Miracles: Lessons Learned from a Surgeon's Experience with Exceptional Patients* (New York: Harper & Row, 1986). It is an encouraging book to read during earlier stages of diminishment, for it helps create very healthy attitudes in dealing with sickness. It is especially relevant in blessing your medications.

Stage 2. Inner Resistance

1. Pierre Teilhard de Chardin, "The Meaning and Constructive Value of Suffering," in *Teilhard de Chardin: Pilgrim of the Future*, ed. Neville Braybrooke, trans. Noel Lindsay (New York: Seabury Press, 1964), 23.

2. Ibid., 84.

3. See the section "Spiritual Practices: The Fundamental Choice for Health" in chap. 1, p. 33.

PART TWO: Stages of Transformation

1. Some sufferers may realize that they are already in stage 3. Certain ones automatically enter the process at the stages of transformation because their sickness or diminishment has no cure, given the present state of medicine. They must cope with it as long as they live. Consider, for example, those with diabetes, chronic Lyme disease, HIV/AIDS, Parkinson's disease, Crohn's disease, psoriasis, or hemophilia; also those who are faced with a lifelong mental or physical disability such as schizophrenia, bipolar disorder, drug addiction, blindness, deafness, paralysis, Downs syndrome, dwarfism, multiple sclerosis, cerebral palsy, loss of limbs, or other physical challenges that tend to produce social ostracism, public embarrassment, or shame.

Stage 3. Prayer

1. John Henry Cardinal Newman, *Meditations and Devotions of the Late Cardinal Newman* (New York: Longmans, Green & Co., 1907), 301.

Stage 4. Patience

1. Joyce Meyer, *Battlefield of the Mind* (Brentwood, TN: Warner Faith, 2002), 230.

2. Rainer Maria Rilke, *Letters to a Young Poet*, trans. M. D. Herter Norton, rev. ed. (New York: W. W. Norton & Company, 1993), 27.

3. Henri J. M. Nouwen, "A Spirituality of Waiting: Being Alert to God's Presence in Our Lives," *Weavings* 1 (1986): 9.

4. Anne Lamott, *Bird by Bird: Some Instructions on Writing and Life* (New York: Knopf Doubleday, 2007), 99.

Stage 5. Choice

1. Teilhard de Chardin, *The Divine Milieu* (New York: Harper Collins, 1965), 75–76.

2. Carlo Maria Martini, *Journeying with the Lord: Reflections for Everyday* (New York: Alba House, 1987).

3. Henry J. M. Nouwen, *The Inner Voice of Love: A Journey through Anguish to Freedom* (New York: Doubleday, 1996), 91.

PART THREE: Stages of Union

Stage 6. Communion

1. Pierre Teilhard de Chardin, *The Divine Milieu* (New York: Harper Collins, 1965), 86.

Stage 7. Fidelity

1. You can find an example of Teilhard's experience of stage 7 described well in his "Mass on the World" in *Hymn of the Universe* (New York: Harper & Row, 1961).

2. Teilhard de Chardin, *The Divine Milieu*, 85.

3. Review and reflect on the "Prayer Form: A Prayer of Gratitude" in chap. 4, p. 73.

4. Mother Teresa, "Nobel Lecture," December 11, 1979, The Nobel Peace Prize, 1979. Cf. http://www.nobelprize.org/nobel_prizes/peace/laureates/1979/teresa–lecture.html.

Index of
Spiritual Practices

Index of
Prayer Forms

Books in the
Teilhard *Explained* Series
By Louis M. Savary and Patricia H. Berne